POETIC VOYAGES
BRISTOL VOL II

Edited by Lucy Jeacock

First published in Great Britain in 2002 by
YOUNG WRITERS
Remus House,
Coltsfoot Drive,
Peterborough, PE2 9JX
Telephone (01733) 890066

HB ISBN 0 75433 420 1
SB ISBN 0 75433 421 X

To Jean & David
With love from the
author of What is...
.. Earth

Love from

Chloë
xxxx

FOREWORD

Young Writers was established in 1991 with the aim
to promote creative writing in children, to make
reading and writing poetry fun.

This year once again, proved to be a tremendous
success with over 88,000 entries received nationwide.

The Poetic Voyages competition has shown us the
high standard of work and effort that children are
capable of today. It is a reflection of the teaching
skills in schools, the enthusiasm and creativity they
have injected into their pupils shines clearly within
this anthology.

The task of selecting poems was therefore a difficult
one but nevertheless, an enjoyable experience. We
hope you are as pleased with the final selection in
Poetic Voyages Bristol Vol II as we are.

CONTENTS

Bank Leaze Primary School

Paul Edwards	18
Charlotte Mason	18
Michael Lammas	19
Charlotte Andrews	19
Claire Doak	20
Hannah Blake	20
Vanessa Lammas	21
Jordan Beail	22
Lucy Bakehouse	22
Mark Ware	23
Nico George	23
Jordan Britton	24
Hazel Capstick	24
Junior Feltham	25
Jenny Hill	25

Bristol Steiner Waldorf School

Sarah Chorley	26

Cameley Primary School

Lauren Gilbert	26
Jenny Ajderian	27
Kaytie Pinder	28
Grace Wilson	28
Chris Merrick	29
Zoe Walton	29
Katie Bowes	30
Robert Harrison	30
Miles Luxton	30
Kim-Ling	31
Sascha May	31

Chandag Junior School

Michael Cork	31
Jeffrey Downie	32
Natalie Mott	32
Alice Pollitt	33

Jake McGann	56
Jessica Lambert	56
William Rich	57
Rohan Coates	58
Joe Passafaro	58
Oliver Gallaugher	59
Alice Caird	60
Imogen Parkes	60
Rachel Baker	61
Kim Richardson	61
Loretta Holt	62

Clutton Primary School

Arron Hotchkins	62
Sam Gilbert	63
George Parfitt	63
Matthew Lacey	64
Keith Marwood	65
Ross Beecroft	66
Laura Densley	66
Holly Graham	67
Matthew Sparks	68
Joanna Withers	68
Victor Higgins	69
Vanessa Withey	69
Richard Lawlor	70
Christopher Brent	70
Alice Tanner	71
Ellen Wickes	72
Rachel Bennett	72
Kelly Hedges	73
Daniel Raisbeck	73
James Tremlett	74
May Alexander	75
Catherine Stenner	76
Victoria Jenkins	76
Sophie Howe	76

Damien Davies	77
Steven Taylor	77
Ross Dunford	78
Lily Holloway	78
Ruby Cook & Jennifer Stone	79

Colston's Girls' School

Emily May	80
Jade Jetley	80
Lesley-Ann Curtis	81
Rasheena Malik	82
Elly Herbert	82
Daisy Woods	83
Sarah Stephenson-White	83
Alys Fletcher	84
Sarah Vernon	84
Jane Holmes	85
Hannah Vallin	86
Alison Windsor	87
Rosie Garrard	88
Sophie Weston	88
Zuwena Reid-Bailey	89
Florence McClelland	90
Hannah White	91
Charlotte Lonsdale	92

Coniston Primary School

Kelly Ware	92
Kaylee Cullinan	93
Alex Diaper	94
Kristian Barrs	94
Lorraine Allen	95
Ben Morris	95

Court-de-Wyck Primary School

Sammy Martin & Louise Ball	96
Chloe Headdon & Ashley Johns	96

Golden Valley School

Matt Pilgrim	97
Ben Leaman	98
Danielle Horler	99
Lucy Smith	100
Emily Gingell	101
Luke Jenkins	102
Ben Tucker	102
Joshua Bagnall	103
Tiffany Whitchurch	104
Jack Newton	104
James Smith	105
Zoe Lewis	106
Ella Randall	107
Emma Jarosz	108
Tamsyn Whitchurch	108
Gemma Ostler	109
Lucy Cockerton	110
Amiee Dowden	111
Claire Malton	112
Hannah Searcy	113
Jade Whymark	114
Hallam Merryweather	114
Dominique Graeme-Wilson	115
Rhys Matson	116
Joe Hastings	116
Gemma Howard	117
Sophie Brooks	118
James Minett	118
Helena Ryan	119
Lucy Parry	120
Emily Perry	120
Alexander Child	121
Phoebe Pring	122
Ellie Smith	123
Christopher Wall	124

Sheryl Thompson	198
Paul Timms	198
Sophie Kethro	199
Lisa Marie Read	199
Nick Miller	200
Rachael Ware	200
Ryan Hale	201
Lydia Smith	201
Laura Ford	202

Silverhill School

Amy Wheeler	203
Joshua Reason	204
Joseph Tregear	204
Russell Avenin	205
Christopher Brown	205
Francesca Norris	206
Gareth Knowles	206
Gregory Sturge	207
Edward Bourns	207
Joshua Oware	208
Jessica Milsom	208
Nazia Mulla	209
Catherine Perry	210
Nicole Crompton	210
Jack Maddox	211
Joanna Norris	212
Oliver Shepherd	213
Charlotte Macleod	214
Samantha McCouig	214
Joshua Goddard	215
Edward Moyse	216
Amber Thomas	216
Thomas Drury	217
Robbie Williamson	217
Samuel Hobbs	218
Charlotte Lacey	218
Alastair Bradley	219

The Poems

UNTITLED

I started my voyage on a cold winter's night,
In the starry sky, the moon shone bright.
We left the house at the end of the day
With my dog and a torch to light the way.

We were going away in a sailing ship
The men drank beer, I had a sip.
We had a feast, a big one too
Was I really here? Was this voyage true?

We sailed on, very fast
I saw some sharks swimming past.
There was a storm, we could not go
The waves tossed the ship to and fro.

We found an island, a little one,
The captain was tense, he had a gun.
We sat on the island and thought of a plot
There was a cross, X marks the spot!

We dug and dug throughout the day
The tide came and swept the sand away.
We heard a grunt from down below,
A monster! Should we stay or go?

We wanted the treasure and decided to fight.
The monster was ugly, a terrible sight.
It was over at last, we heard a groan
We were victorious! And on our way home.

Amelia Tennant (9)
Ashley Down Junior School

TIGER TIGER

Tiger tiger running through the swamp,
Tiger tiger stomp! stomp! stomp!
Tiger tiger running really fast,
Tiger tiger he's never last,
Tiger tiger lying down,
Tiger tiger ain't a clown,
Tiger tiger catch his prey,
Tiger tiger hunts every day,
Tiger tiger has lots of cubs,
Tiger tiger find a tree and rubs,
Tiger tiger eats loads and loads of food,
Tiger tiger always in a good mood,
Tiger tiger hardly ever sad,
Tiger tiger he's never bad,
Tiger tiger their favourite is deer,
Tiger tiger they drink water that's clear,
Tiger tiger they are orange and black,
Tiger tiger think you are a snack,
Tiger tiger like humans they twist and bend,
Tiger tiger now this is the end!

Alex Mandry (9)
Ashley Down Junior School

JOURNEY

J   oy passes by as the days grow longer
O   verhead winds pass by
U   nion Jack flag flies high
R   emembrance Day. Just comes and goes, no time to stop and think.
N   earer and nearer the last of my journey comes to an end.
E   ver more cold, the nights get
Y   et now my journey is over.

Amanda Goodall (10)
Ashley Down Junior School

MY VOYAGE

I started my voyage on a cold winter's night
Up in the sky, the moon shone bright.
All we had was a piece of pie
So off we went, my dog and I.
Slowly I pushed off my boat
Then when it was off, it started to float.
My dog got scared and started to hide
'Don't be scared' I quietly sighed.
For a moment I thought the moon was our guide
But then it also started to hide.
We carried on, both of us alone
But then my dog wanted a bone.
I gave him one and then I found
Finally I was there
And then I saw it
The thing I came to see
I got my notebook and pen out
And drew the crocodile, just he.

Katie Dilleigh (8)
Ashley Down Junior School

SPACE

I'm flying through space at the speed of light
I'm travelling to the moon it's very bright.
I'm gong past stars and planets
And I'm getting closer now.
I look at the Milky Way and see a flying cow
Now I'm at the moon plodding about, I see an alien
I give it a shout,
He gives me a zap gun
I fly back home to try it out.

Luke Thorne (10)
Ashley Down Junior School

A VOYAGE INTO SPACE

5 4 3 2 1 *blast-off!*
As the world gets smaller and smaller
We're being blasted off into space
Past the planets, past the stars,
Whizzing past Jupiter
Never stopping.
We're being hurtled past the Milky Way
Hurtled past the stars.
But now
We have reached
Our destination
It's Pluto.
5 4 3 2 1 *touchdown!*
We are here now
Mission accomplished.
We see Charon
But little else.
It's time to go
Back to the rocket
5 4 3 2 1 *blast-off!*
Right past Mars
Earth comes into sight
5 4 3 2 1 *touchdown!*
We are back home!

Chris Maddix (8)
Ashley Down Junior School

THE DEEP DARK CAVE

Walking through the deep dark cave
rough though it be
Shining a torch everywhere.

Then I see something
as thick and as black as coal
turning my head then it's gone.

Walking through the scary cave
touching the walls to help my way
looking through the dark mist.

Then I bump into something
hard and rough
Saved though I be.

I see a light
the thing in front of me
was only my dad

He gave me a hug
and gave me a kiss
he took me outside and told me

'Don't go out
Without telling me.'

Jack H-W (10)
Ashley Down Junior School

THE MAGIC CRYSTAL

I walk out of my wooden house
And view the lovely blue and white water
Splashing on the rocks
I slide down the seaweed rocks
And see the orange and yellow sun
I slide into the warm sand
I walk along the sand
It crackles at my feet
I see a little crystal
Sleeping in the sand
I gently pick it up
I look around I am in a cave
The walls are covered in soot
I see a ladder, slowly I climb it
At the top I seed fifty zombies
I see a crystal, I pick it up
And I am back in my cosy bed.

Callum Campbell (9)
Ashley Down Junior School

MY JOURNEY

Sitting on the seat
Propellers going round
Going on the runway
We'll soon be off the ground.

The countries are all tiny
They're going past too fast
I'd stay here for ages
How long will this flight last?

Some people laughing
Others have a drink
I'm just sitting here
I'm trying hard to think.

We're slowing down, we're almost there
It's almost time to land
Time's flown by, it's just not fair
Now we've touched the ground.

Louise Sutherland (10)
Ashley Down Junior School

MY IN-SERVICE!

I woke up and my voyage began
I wiped the sleep from my eyes
All the way down the stairs I ran
To find two great big pies
Were they for me, of course they were
For me to take out to sea
To splat them at the enemy pirates
Then they would all look at me
They'd lift their patches off their eyes
And send their parrots in the air
But they'll send back those two big pies
With no crumbs to spare
All I can remember, is it all being settled
And somehow being all a-play
Then I woke up with my mum beside me
And I started my in-service day.

Sheriden Russell (11)
Ashley Down Junior School

AFRAID

Witch
Cat
Ghost
Bat
Frankenstein's monster
Black rat.

Vampire
Minotaur
Skeleton
Loud roar
Glowing eyes
Bodiless claw.

Monsters face
Eerie light
Cyclops
Dark night
Haunted house
Terrible fright.

Eve Phillips (9)
Ashley Down Junior School

COLOURS

As red as a rose
As green as grass
As yellow as the sun
As blue as the sky
As brown as mud
And as orange as a current.

Danielle Thornton (9)
Ashley Down Junior School

NIGHTMARE IN THE SEA

Waves splash
And I'm in a dash.

Across the sea
My friend and me

It brings us to the sand
In a deserted land.

Back in the sea
My friend and me

Across to the shore
There's my mum
Looks like she's been in a war
A war I cry.

Is she OK, better check
Then I wake up
I'm glad there's no more.

Katie Newton (9)
Ashley Down Junior School

I WISH I WAS A BIRD

I wish I was a bird,
Journeying through the sunlit sky,
High above golden cornfields, waving in the wind.
Dipping down to the babbling brook,
Breeze flowing, past my wings.
Clouds like floating fluffy sheep,
And back to nest
To hungry chicks.

Christopher Lock (9)
Ashley Down Junior School

LIFE

The voyage of life
A special one too
We all have it
Me and you.

The path of life,
Has hiccups and problems
But dreams are uncovered
Or precious gems to make your life unique
Until it ends.

For the voyage of life
Your body is your kit.
So please try your best to make the most of it.

Bryony Budd (8)
Ashley Down Junior School

THE ADVENTURES OF ISABEL

Isabel met an enormous bear
Isabel Isabel did not care
The bear was hungry, the bear was raucous
The bear's big mouth was cavernous
The bear said, 'Isabel Isabel pleased to meet you
Isabel Isabel now I'll eat you.'
Isabel Isabel did not scream or scurry
Before she had 'had' sweetcorn and curry
Then she ate the bear all up hurry.

Paris Olivia Vassell (8)
Ashley Down Junior School

A JOURNEY OF LIFE

Life is like a trip across the ocean
Sometimes rough,
Sometimes calm.
But just when you feel like jumping overboard,
There is always a new horizon
And always a beautiful sunset.
And at the end of your journey
You drift
       into
            calm
                 waters.

Samuel Goodbrand (9)
Ashley Down Junior School

A TRIP TO FRANCE

I'm on a trip to France
I'm on a rocking boat
I feel as if I'm going to puke
I feel the boat is going to tip
As I get further, waves get more stronger
I'm worried
At last the waves calm down
The sun starts to shine
Ah I'm calm
I'm on my way
Yeah I'm there!

Daniel Berry (9)
Ashley Down Junior School

A Week Of Friendship

On Monday I visited the zoo and I played with my best friend Lou.
On Tuesday I walked up to the park and I saw my good friend Mark.
On Wednesday I went to the forest and I made a new friend Maurice.
On Thursday I cycled to get some cash and I bumped into
my friend Tash.
On Friday I drove to the beach and I saw my friend Kalich.
On Saturday I ran out in the rain and I saw my friend Jane.
On Sunday I stayed at home and I felt very alone.

Lauren Russ-Constant (8)
Ashley Down Junior School

Untitled

As I dive beneath the waves,
They enfold me in their tender grip,
Yet draw me down into the shadowy depths.

Life is born from those paranormal shadows,
All life upon Earth must one day return,
And swim amongst the wonders of our world.

I see many tiny shoals of tiny fish,
That hold me captive with their dance,
Here time seems to come and go.

But as the water pulls me farther down,
I look up to the light,
Then go down, down to the unknown.

Charlotte Maddix (10)
Ashley Down Junior School

A SAILOR'S TRIP

The orange sun reflecting on the sea
Dolphins leaping gracefully over the sunset
Drifting slowly on the calm sea
The boat rocks gently
The world getting ready for sleep.

The noise of a whale awakes me with a start
The call echoes through the ship
I look across the shimmering sea
A whale is struggling in a net
Set last evening for fish.

Me and the crew set off in the speedboat
We slide and glide across the ocean
To save the injured whale
I jump from the boat and come to rescue
It wriggles and squirms, but at last it's free.

My eyes suddenly open
My hands are dry, not cold and wet
I stare out the window, the stars are winking
I switch on the light, there's no whining whale
Phew, it was only a dream.

Vicky Brown (9)
Ashley Down Junior School

SOUNDS

Sounds, sounds everywhere, sounds, sounds everywhere.
In my drum, in my guitar, in my piano, that's where they are.
They're in a chirp, they're in a coo, they're in a twitter
They're in a moo.
Sounds, sounds, everywhere, sounds, sounds everywhere.

James Oakes (10)
Ashton Vale Primary School

LISTEN!

Listen!
(What can you hear?)
Children crying tears, as blue as the sea,
Dogs climbing frantically up trees,
Grandads pushing little babies,
Cats chasing flying fleas.

Listen!
(What can you hear?)
Teacher shouting at children when they're naughty,
Little scratches on the blackboard,
Children laughing in the corridor,
Adverbs won the winning cup.

Listen!
(What can you hear?)
Listen!
(What can . . .)
Shhhhhhhhhh! Don't say a thing
Listen!
(What can you hear?)
. . . *Everything.*

Faye McCarthy (8)
Ashton Vale Primary School

FA CUP FINAL

What a football match this is so far,
Some of the home fans are going to the bar.
The home fans have been singing all the way through,
The away fans are giving them a *boo*
The home team went 1-0 up,
The away team thought they were going to win the FA Cup.

Connor Flicker (9)
Ashton Vale Primary School

LOOK!

Look!
(What can you see?)
City fans waving scarves like the wind itself,
A swaying mass of bobbing heads,
Crowds leaping like headless chickens,
Goal is scored, by the reds.

Look!
(What can you see?)
Poppies as red as blood,
Leaves swaying in a gentle breeze,
Caterpillars like juicy candy,
A gathering of swarming bumblebees.

Look!
(What can you see?)
Children singing in the hall,
A bully staring at me,
Teachers sitting like they're glued to a chair and
A teacher, like he.

Look!
(What can you see?)
Stop don't even blink.
Look!
(What can you see?)
Everything.

Daniel Lock (9)
Ashton Vale Primary School

TULIP THE PERFUME MONSTER

Tulip is a perfume monster,
She loves all kinds of flowers,
For she has many great powers,
She's smellier than all the flowers put together,
She always loves the sunny weather,
She's quieter than many flowers asleep,
When nobody's looking she rides on the back of sheep,
She's more intelligent than the boss, God,
She is who all the flowers prod,
Tulip's best friend is Katy,
For she is her only matey,
She's prettier than a beauty queen,
Every time she steps out she's been seen,
She's as graceful as a swan,
She gets blamed for what she hasn't done,
She's as tall as a sunflower,
Oh yeah! she has power.

Natasha Thomas (8)
Ashton Vale Primary School

MOUSE

Cheese-eater
Finger-biter
Fast-runner
Water-drinker
Bar-chewer
Fur-ball

Jessica Perry (10)
Ashton Vale Primary School

THE FRIENDLY MONSTER

The friendly monster is slower than the most sluggish snail,
Dumber than the silliest sheep,
As loud as an hen laying an egg,
Hairier than a monkey,
Smellier than a dustbin filled with rubbish,
As happy as a person,
Fat as an elephant
But he is as friendly as a puppy,
And most of all wants to be your friend.

Kelsey Pearce (8)
Ashton Vale Primary School

RAPPING THE TEACHERS

Mrs Cross is the boss
Around the school
She's so cool.

Mr T,
He's so good with ICT.

Mrs Lee,
She gets on with me.

Mr Owen,
He's so good at writing poems.

Mrs Cross is the boss,
Around the school,
She's so cool.

Toni Smith (9)
Ashton Vale Primary School

CAT

Mouse-eater
Fish-eater
Evening-wanderer
Finger-licker
Engine-purrer.

Hayley Branson (9)
Ashton Vale Primary School

MONSTERS

They're creepy, they're crawly,
they're on the loose at night,
From vampires to zombies,
they all give you a fright.
Some are big, some are small,
no matter what, I run from them all.
Some live in the cupboards,
some hide under your bed.
However I'm not scared because
mine has just been fed!

Paul Edwards (8)
Bank Leaze Primary School

COLOURS

Roses are red
I love my bed.
Grass is green
I love to scream.
Sky is blue
I've got the flu.

Charlotte Mason (8)
Bank Leaze Primary School

ROCKETS

Rockets go up
and down
day by day
up
and down.
From
Earth to Mars,
or
to the moon.
They
can be red
black
and white
and they come
in
all shapes
and sizes.

Michael Lammas (8)
Bank Leaze Primary School

JACK FROST

Wherever he walks
Ice goes around
Over the ground.

He makes patterns
On the wall
He flies up to the window
And makes sure everyone is asleep
And blows ice patterns.

Charlotte Andrews (7)
Bank Leaze Primary School

ROBBERY

Sitting at home
Thinking nothing's wrong
While people outside
Are helping themselves to my mum's car.

Taking the stereo
Off they run
To sell it to make money
For drugs or something else.

The next morning we wake up
To take my niece out
It's her first birthday
What a horrible way to start.

It's a good job we have insurance
Otherwise we would be stuck
I hope the police catch the people
And my niece will have a better second birthday.

Claire Doak (10)
Bank Leaze Primary School

IT'S WINTERTIME

Cold foggy morning
I can hear Mum calling
Too warm to get up
Too cold to go out.

Quick let in the cat
It's been out all night
Cold paws, frozen whiskers
Next time you go out,
Put on your hat.

Time for school
We'll have to walk
Car's frozen over
More time to talk.

Hannah Blake (10)
Bank Leaze Primary School

I'M A ROBBER

Sitting in my car, waiting for people to leave their cars.
So when they go I strike and do what I love to do.
I smash the window,
Look around
To check that no one is watching me.
In goes my arm,
I snatch the bag,
Yes! I got it hooray hooray!

The poor people I robbed,
They probably miss their property.
I have a new place to stay the night
The house keys were in the bag I took
There was also money, loads of money.
I'd best hide my identity
The cops will be after me now.

I'm at the house,
Looking through the phone book,
I think I'll make some prank calls,
That should be fun.
Being a robber is fun
I think I'll be one forever.

Vanessa Lammas (10)
Bank Leaze Primary School

WINTER

In the winter it is freezing.
All the time I am sneezing.
When the snowflakes start to fall
They all land on our wall.

In the winter the trees are bare
All the children stand and stare.
Make a snowman in a field
But they are very hard to build.

In the winter I wrap up warm.
Just in case of a snowstorm.
I put on my scarf, my gloves and my hat.
Then I go and chase the cat.

In the winter comes Christmas time.
When we all drink lots of wine.
There are lots of presents under the tree
I have fun with my family.

Jordan Beail (8)
Bank Leaze Primary School

THERE WAS ONCE A KNIGHT

There was once a knight
who was brave and bold.
He wasn't at all very old.
He pulled out his sword
and drank funny water
just to rescue the captain's daughter.
Why did the knight pull out his sword?
I just guess to impress the mighty lord.

Lucy Bakehouse (10)
Bank Leaze Primary School

WAR!

The guns go off
The war begins.
All around me
I hear screams and crying of children.
Bombs dropping from the sky.
Making loud noises as they reach the ground.
People die
From guns and grenades.
The blood on the ground
Represents the poppy.
The war ends.
And all you can hear are screams for help
From all the people that died for us.

Mark Ware (10)
Bank Leaze Primary School

THE VOLCANO

Shaking my whole entire island
Gas floating in the sky
Making people suffer and die
Acid burning houses.

Lava whooshing down
Mountains hitting houses
Making people turn into rock
Ponds and swimming pools are
Bubbling and spitting.

People running and crying
With pets running too.

Nico George (11)
Bank Leaze Primary School

Trees!

One day a seed was in the ground
Slowly growing with no sound
The roots pop out and spread out wide
In the corner and by the side
Out comes the stem really tall
Thin and long just like a straw
Then it grows into a trunk
The branches bend like they are drunk
On the branches forms a tiny bud
As the roots grow stronger through the mud
I wonder what it's going to be
An apple or a pear tree?
I'm going to have a house up there
With my sister and her teddy bear
I know we will have lots of fun
As the branches reach the sun
I'm going to call this tree the biggest thing
                    you will ever see.

Jordon Britton (9)
Bank Leaze Primary School

Going On Holiday

We travel by car.
I hope it's not far.
When I go on holiday, I lie in the sun
I swim in the sea or the pool.
I think it is pretty cool.
We go to the beach and get sandy feet,
And later on I go to the disco
and get to the beat.

Hazel Capstick (8)
Bank Leaze Primary School

A SPACE ADVENTURE

The countdown begins.
There's no turning back.
Soon I will be blasted into space.
With silence, not even a rat.
Here it goes, the ship starts to shake
Clouds of smoke fill the air.
Sweat trickles down my face.
The doors are firmly shut.
There is no escape.
Up I go, I can feel the ship shaking.

I'm there.
The ship is smoothly gliding through space.
In the distance, I can see the enormous golden sun.
Beep, beep, beep.
That's the alarm I'm losing fuel,
I'm going to land back on earth,
Ready to tell everyone about my fantastic journey in space.

Junior Feltham (11)
Bank Leaze Primary School

THE WIND

The wind flew past me as I walked by.
The wind is waving, backwards and forwards.
The wind is cold and strong.
The wind is quiet as can be.
The wind is wailing at me.
It flies by me as I walk down the street.

Jenny Hill (10)
Bank Leaze Primary School

THE ELEPHANT

Long leathery legs, long swaying trunk
Big beautiful ears, and long ivory tusks.
Swaying along with its big and wise herd
Walking through jungles that have never been heard.
Stopping at rivers for a drink and a wash
In the shade of a tree it softly sleeps
Always watching for a twitch or a roar
At dawn they walk with their young at their side
Starting a new day at the sunrise.

Sarah Chorley (10)
Bristol Steiner Waldorf School

MATILDA

Matilda has a furry pink nose,
But no way does she smell like a beautiful rose,
BT is her mother; together they are mad,
Since we've had Matilda she has been extremely bad.
Matilda likes to watch telly,
She always used to poo on Dad's welly,
Now Matilda goes out at night,
But it doesn't stop her from having a fight.
Matilda likes to listen to clocks,
She always has and always will like socks.
She sometimes likes to sit in the car,
When she's outside she doesn't go far.
It's said that cats like rats,
Matilda doesn't, she's more interested with hats.
Matilda likes to play with string,
She goes mad when she hears a ping.

Lauren Gilbert (9)
Cameley Primary School

FADING SHADOWS IN THE NIGHT

Fading shadows in the night,
on the walls give me a fright.
Baring teeth and dripping fangs,
with ears I sense a clang!
Turning round and staring full,
I see the image of a bull.
I look again and see myself,
It's just a mouse upon a shelf.

Walking upwards on the stairs,
recovering from severe scares.
I sense I do, I sense again
With feet I sense a pain.
I look full down and see a crown
resting on my foot.
It feels like it is cooked it does,
full pain upon my foot.

Fading shadows in the night,
On the walls give me a fright
Baring teeth and dripping fangs,
With ears I sense a clang!
Wake up sweating in my bed
Now the pain is in my head
I'll never never dream again
About that little red hen.
About that little red hen.

Jenny Ajderian (9)
Cameley Primary School

THE SUN IS A . . .

The sun is a yellow yo-yo without the string.
The sun is a juicy lemon without the juice.
The sun is a yellow ball without the bounce.
The sun is a yellow lion without the roar.
The sun is a yellow parrot without its beak.
The sun is a pot of yellow paint without the paintbrush.
The sun is a yellow balloon without the air.
The sun is a yellow hat without the head.
The sun is a yellow book without the writing.
That is what the sun is.

Kaytie Pinder (10)
Cameley Primary School

THE SEA IS . . .

The sea is
A gigantic bath of glistening water
A set of blue pom-poms
A blue woolly jumper
A whale swimming softly, singing its song
Bluebells peeping but petals fall
Tomorrow's rain falling on the snow
A small bridge standing all alone over a river.

That's what the sea is.

Grace Wilson (9)
Cameley Primary School

TORCH IN THE SKY

M y torch in the sky
O rbits my beautiful Earth that I call home
O bserving the solar system's peaceful atmosphere
N octurnal sparkling stars
L ighting the quiet dead of night
I magine the world without the torch
G littering in the big swirl of gas
H ome to no one, or is it?
T winkling lonely in the midnight sky.

Chris Merrick (9)
Cameley Primary School

CHOCOLATE

C hocolate is my favourite food
H ow tasty it is, oh so good
O n my glistening tongue
C alories are high I know
O n the hips it goes
L oved by almost everyone
A t any time of day
T ry it if you dare
E at it but *beware!*

Zoe Walton (8)
Cameley Primary School

THE NIGHT IS . . .

The night is a dark crow swiftly swooping over the world.
The night is a black carpet being laid on the sky.
The night is a spoonful of marmite being spread over the planets.
The night is a black bag covering the light.
The night is a pair of black shoes dancing over the sun.
The night is a field of black horses trotting beneath the moon.
That's what I think the night is.

Katie Bowes (9)
Cameley Primary School

HOMELESSNESS

How I live I don't know
Oh I want a home
My family doesn't love me
Even animals don't like me
Live or die
Empty tummy
So I live
So I die, no one cares.

Robert Harrison (10)
Cameley Primary School

THE STAR IS

The star is a blob of glitter in the sky
The star is someone smiling, burning bright
The star is a deserted planet
The star is a shining thing
The star is a world of peace
That is what a star is.

Miles Luxton (9)
Cameley Primary School

THE DEEP BLUE SEA IS A . . .

The sea is a
>Huge puddle with ships
>Smooth and gentle
>A jumper without any holes
>Big patch of blue snow
>Big swimming pool
>Big bowl of water
>Wonderful bath with blue water
>Watery gentle blue sky.

Kim-Ling (9)
Cameley Primary School

SWEETS

S   weets are very good to eat
W hen you want a big treat
E   veryone enjoys the taste
E   ven better than toothpaste
T   eeth become rotten I know
S   o enjoy the taste and away we go.

Sascha May (9)
Cameley Primary School

FROST

F   abulous frost, it is full of bitter air
R   ough like a winter blizzard
O   h how cold it is, it feels like ice cubes
S   till the cold winter blizzard stays
T   errible fearsome nip of the ice pins you down.

Michael Cork (9)
Chandag Junior School

OUR ENVIRONMENT

Trees stretch high,
Like lookout towers,
While the grass thrives down below.

The roaring tractor,
With huge teeth,
Ploughs the field and eats the grass.

Roads wind away
Meandering like streams,
So why do we pollute it,
Like a broken toy?

Jeffrey Downie (9)
Chandag Junior School

THE COUNTRYSIDE

Fields and hills
Like a patchwork quilt.
Rivers flowing,
Wild flowers growing,
Tractors ploughing
The fields.
Cows grazing,
People lazing,
In the midday sun.
Birds glide,
Deers hide,
Foxes search and hunt
In the countryside.

Natalie Mott (9)
Chandag Junior School

MY POETIC VOYAGE

High
So high
Higher than the clouds in the sky.
Oh what's that I think it's an alien!
My tummy is jumping like a bouncy beach ball
My heart is pounding like it's going to come
                                out of my body.

It comes towards me, it's small and green
Three eyes on its purple head, spots and three antenna
I feel a touch of panic I'm so frightened.
What can I do?
I have to do something but what can I do?
I must go now
Zoom.

Alice Pollitt (7)
Chandag Junior School

MY VOYAGE

I am sailing on the sea
the misty blue waves all
crashing on me with fish all around me.

I can see the grey grey cliffs
I can also see lots of ships
lots of fishermen on the shore
and then there was a storm!

Lightning thrashed and the waves crashed
and fish jumped from all directions
the fishermen went home
and it started to pour.

Timothy Aitken (8)
Chandag Junior School

THE COUNTRYSIDE

T rees swaying,
H ares racing,
E very day, cows grazing silently, in the meadow.

C hildren running through the lush, green grass,
O xen ploughing the fields,
U nder the trees, shadows lurk
N oiseless and dark.
T rees stand, like soldiers on duty.
R ivers bubbling gently over stones,
Y oung chicks pecking at grain,
S carecrow in tatters, from the wind and rain.
I vy bushes, as sharp as knives, surrounded by
D aisies and clover,
E verywhere, green fields and meadows.

Billy Arnold (9)
Chandag Junior School

COME INTO MY PRIVATE DEN

Come into my private den
Come on in and have a sneaky peek in
Smell my lovely, tasty cake and my pretty
flowers in a vase
Come on in, please come on in.

And yes you can look in my hiding places
And help me out in my dance routine
You can pick the game we play
And look in my secret diary.

Come on into my private den
Come on in, please come on in.

Angharad Gravell (8)
Chandag Junior School

WHAT AM I?

Silence . . .
As I twirl round the world like a giant whirlwind
As I find my way to the North Pole and beyond

Silence . . .
As I roll over the clouds like a person rolling in some sand
As I hide away through the sunny day.

Silence . . .
As I catch your hat and throw it about!
As I throw you up and away through the windy day.

What am I?

Dawn Bodman (8)
Chandag Junior School

FROST

Children have fun,

While they walk to school sliding along.

At the end of school
They are out in the frost,
When they come in they say,
The ice is so nippy and slippy outside.
Your feet are sore and your lips are raw,
On Monday the frost will all melt away.

Now in the class,
Looking so sad,
They lookout the window and see the frost man.

Josephine Parish (9)
Chandag Junior School

COME ON INTO MY MAGICAL CAVE

Come on into my magical cave
Come on in and have a glimpse in
Taste some of my rock sparkle water and eat
                                    my rock cubes
Come on in, please come on in.

And yes you can swim in my secret river
And slide down my magical waterfall
You can climb my trees that reach the sky
And dig in my dungeons.

O yes you can play in my secret sandpit
And fly on my magical falcon
You can paddle in my jacuzzi
And play with my hound.

Come on into my magical cave
Come on in, please come on in.

Alex Joyce (8)
Chandag Junior School

MY POETIC VOYAGE

On a ship
Stormy and windy
I'm cold, cold like ice.
Waves crash on the rocks
Ahead the sandy shore.

It's over
Into the silvery ocean deep and gloomy.
There's a cave - I go in
Seaweed a silvery green.
I leave.

Rush up to have a breath
Go down
See the glittering sunshine upon me.
Now it's time to go on ship.

Victoria Bailey (7)
Chandag Junior School

MY POETIC VOYAGE

Zooming up to space
Up up I'm going
Each yard more gloomy
Suddenly the rocket doors open.

Space helmet on
Carefully, step outside
A cold rush of air
Runs through my lungs.

Standing there
There's an alien.
Its scabbed hands clutches my shoulders,
Its rattling breath comes from its hooded head.

I wouldn't dare see what's beyond its hood
But I can't resist it.
I lift it up.
Suddenly my heart starts pounding
Like never before.

It has no eyes
Instead a huge mouth
Ten antenna and three sharp teeth.
Suddenly I turn and run, but where?

Alex Price (8)
Chandag Junior School

COME INTO MY DREAM WORLD

Come into my dream world
Come on in and take a peek through the lime green door
You can taste my lollipops and see my tree with golden leaves
Come on in, please come on in.

And yes you can see the nests that the birds make
With colourful diamonds in my purple and blue trees
And go in my desert where the sand is sherbet
And the rocks are jelly babies
You can find bits of wine gums and the trees bounce like kangaroos.

Come on into my dream world
Come on in, please come on in.

Sarah Riddoch (8)
Chandag Junior School

MY VOYAGE

My voyage started when I was riding
on an elephant through the jungle
looking for a parrot to put in my cage.

My voyage started when I was walking
through the forest hunting
for a tiger to eat for my tea.

My voyage started when I was fishing
for a cat fish to sell on the market.

My voyage started when I was hunting
for a giraffe to ride on its back and look for a monkey.

My voyage ended when I was on the beach sunbathing
with all the animals.

James Tavener (7)
Chandag Junior School

MY VOYAGE

I am sailing on my boat,
In my little yellow coat,
Looking for the landscapes,
Maybe I will find a green, or maybe yellow landscape.
I am sailing on my boat,
In my little red coat,
Looking for the view
And when I turned my boat I could smell lovely, tasty
stew, coming from the cabin.
Then I said 'that's it no more voyages today.
I will go to sleep instead.'
When I was snoring in the morning I got up and I shouted
'I am in my boat,
Wearing my little blue coat!'

Jessica Scott (7)
Chandag Junior School

MY VOYAGE

I'd like to be in a balloon, high in the sky.
The gentle breeze up there in the warm.
The white clouds would be behind us.
We would put the gas on, then we'd go high, high, high!

We'd stay up there in the freezing night.
The full moon out glittering
but then we might hear the werewolf's howl!

In the morning I would be snoring in the balloon.
We would land a bumpy landing
Then we'd tramp the balloon all down
Ready to pack it up.

Ross Taylor (7)
Chandag Junior School

MY POETIC VOYAGE

We're on a desert island
Far, far away
Pearls and diamonds hidden somewhere
Underneath, underneath
Dig, dig quick, quick, dig, dig, quick, quick.

We've found it, we've found it
Under the sandy depths
An old wooden chest of drawers
Open it, open it, open it quick
We have found pearls and diamonds
We're happy, happy, happy.

We take the treasure slowly, slowly
Back to the boat and then sail back home
We're rich, rich, rich.

Charlotte Miché (7)
Chandag Junior School

MY VOYAGE

Big
Lots of space
Engines, machines making noises
Down to the bottom of the sea
Down we go
Red fish
Blue fish
Seaweed
Octopus
Sharks
Goldfish.

Joe Savage (8)
Chandag Junior School

MY MAGIC BOX

I will put in my box
The first bark of a dog
The glisten of a star
The bang of a firework.

I will put in my box
The sound of the sea rushing towards the shore,
The first splash of a dolphin
A bright colourful rainbow in the deep blue sky.

My box is made of gold,
Its hinges are smooth.

With my box
I will search the jungles,
that have never been seen before.

Rebecca Crane (9)
Chandag Junior School

MY VOYAGE

I've been in a hot air balloon,
past hundreds of stars.
I've travelled through England
I've been to Mars.
In day or night,
I like to fly,
up so very high in the sky.
I look down, down below my feet.
I see the fields full of wheat.

Anneleise Williams (7)
Chandag Junior School

MY VOYAGE

I remember, I remember
when I went to Scotland
the green fields and the little country lanes.
It was not a house, it was a bungalow
I was there with my family.

I remember when I went to Cheddar Caves
the slimy stuff on the walls
and the water on the floor.
It was very cool.

I remember, I remember my old house.
I had a friend over the road
And I had a big garden.
It was the best house in the world.

I remember, I remember going to the beach
It had sandy dunes.
I paddled in the water and I started to sink.
I took three pebbles home but the beach still has some there.

Zoe Williams (8)
Chandag Junior School

THE MAGIC BOX

I will put in my box
A soft sound of a wave on the seashore
A screech of a parrot on a winter night
A purr from a two dimensional cat.

I will put in my box
One drop from each ocean
The first black cloud in the sky
All of the stars from the universe.

My box will be made from gold and silver
The hinges are gold and smooth
And inside it is silver
On the front, a pattern of all the things in it.

Jordan Williams (9)
Chandag Junior School

THE MAGIC BOX

I will put in the box
The first tooth of a baby,
The colours of the rainbow,
and the tip of an ice cold mountain.

I will put in the box
A whisper of an angel
The stars from space
and the colour of the sunset.

I will put in the box
A swish of the first dolphin
A robe made of the finest silk,
and the fire of the red sun.

My box is fashioned from gold and silver,
With squares on the lid.
Its hinges are made out of old bones from a skeleton.

I shall sail in my box on the great high waves
and I will dream in my boat where the crashing waves
                                        take me to shore.

Abigail Cockram (10)
Chandag Junior School

MY MAGIC BOX

I will put in my box
A tenth planet
Another universe
A bronze sun.

I will put in my box
The crash of waves
A rainbow fish
A golden snowman.

I will put in my box
A snowman eating a pepperoni pizza
A kangaroo that talks Chinese
A sudden sting of a strange stingray.

My box is gold with silver stars
It has a multicoloured robe on top of it.
On the box I have a keyhole the colour of
all the colours of the rainbow.
And the key to open it is the colour of gold.

I shall go on exotic adventures to faraway worlds
Where no one has gone before,
And tell everyone about it in my box.

Stephen Hellyer (9)
Chandag Junior School

THE STORM

The thunder haunts the silent night,
like a dragon's fire, a blazing light.

Heart-stopping storm,
for a baby just born.

A terrible fright,
for children at night.

The lightning flashes across the sky
like a flaming oven cooking a pie.

Christopher Read (9)
Chandag Junior School

THE MAGIC BOX

I will put in my box
The darkest yellow sun
A bag of bright pink lollipops
A shooting star over the brightest moon.

I will put in my box
A witching broomstick that goes anywhere
a volcano rumbling when everyone is sleeping
A sharp spike in a dog's paw.

I will put in my box
A new Titanic with big chandeliers
A perfect storm with big waves
A shark's sharp shiny tooth.

My box is fashioned from gold and silver.
The hinges are made out of bronze.
It has bright yellow stars on it
The bottom of it has a very big secret
and it has wheels on the bottom.

I shall play the cello in my box
and on the highest mountain so it will echo.
Then swim in the deepest sea, the colour of the grass.

Nicola Jennings (9)
Chandag Junior School

MY VOYAGE

I remember, I remember
When I went to France,
The ferry had an arcade
And the only drink in the arcade
Was cola in a can.
The only food on the ferry
Was chips, cheeseburgers, hamburgers and salad.
Because I was hungry, I just had chips.

I remember, I remember
When I was in France,
I went to Disneyland
And Martyn got lost.
We found him again in the night
At half-past eleven.
He got told off and nearly smacked
By Grandad Brian.

I remember, I remember
On my last day in France
I saw the Eiffel Tower
But didn't go up.
The tower was big
If I say so myself.
I was in the coach so I couldn't go up.
But if I had the chance I wouldn't go anyway.

Danielle Porritt (8)
Chandag Junior School

THE MAGIC BOX

I would put in my box
a tiny little golden angel
a happy hippopotamus smiling underwater
a phoenix that lays golden eggs.

I would put in my box
a fat fiery fish blowing bubbles
a new ski-bob to ski from the mountain top
a hen diving underwater.

My box is made of stained brown wood
with gold and silver fish on the lid
in the corners are four black friendly dogs.

I would put my box
in a dolphin's mouth
I would ride on the dolphin's back
to a golden beach.

Ashley Jenkins (11)
Chandag Junior School

MY VOYAGE

I remember
a hot air balloon
surprised by the height
I am five feet tall.
Leaving the world behind me.
Birds singing on the way.
High in the sky feeling excited.

Up, up and away

We go.

Anna Hilliar (7)
Chandag Junior School

THE BALLAD OF LITTLE RED RIDING HOOD

Little Red Riding Hood, one day
On the edge of the wood;
In her garden, went out to play
In her red cloak and hood.

That afternoon her mother cried,
'Your grandma is quite ill
Here are some pancakes I have fried,
And also take this pill.'

So, then she set off on her way;
And then who should she meet?
The wolf who wished her a good day,
With a voice kind and sweet.

'Where are you going little girl?'
'My grandma's house' said she.
'Would you like a caramel swirl?'
'Um . . . no' she said quietly.

The wolf said 'How about a race?
You skip, and I will run,
I will move at quite a fast pace,
The winner gets a bun.'

What huge flowers they are she thought,
I'll pick some for Grandma,
I think she'll like them well, she ought,
Oh how pretty they are!

The wolf arrived at destiny,
An hour before the girl.
And ate Gran up excitedly
His tail began to curl.

The girl arrived at the cottage,
And she knocked on the door,
Then entered the little white house,
And then fell upon the floor.

She picked herself up and she said:
'What a big mouth you have!'
'All the better to kiss your forehead,'
The wolf said with a laugh.

'Oh Grandma, what big arms you've got!'
'They'll give big hugs to you.'
'You have quite big teeth have you not?'
He said 'I've quite a few.'

In seconds he'd eaten his fill,
And fell upon the bed,
By now he was feeling quite ill
And he squashed up poor ted.

A passing hunter heard his snores,
And thought something was wrong,
He then followed the marks of claws
And then rang the bell, ding dong!

He walked in and gasped with surprise,
Then slit a hole in Wolf,
The girl jumped out and blinked her eyes
And Gran followed her out.

Louise Mead & Rachel Miché (9)
Chandag Junior School

MY VOYAGE

I am a fisherman
Sailing in the sea
Oh how many
Fish I can see.

I am a fisherman
Setting my sail
Hopefully I will be lucky
And not fail.

I am a fisherman
Catching my fish
Oh will I get home
And have a tasty dish?

I am a fisherman
Ready to go
I have caught
So many
Ho ho ho!

Rhianna Place (8)
Chandag Junior School

ONE SCARED OTTER

Instead of being an otter
I'd rather be a vole
So I wouldn't end up in Mum's casserole.

I'm always really sad
I just can't be a grinner
I'm just too worried about
Ending up as Dad's dinner.

Alastair Stibbs (10)
Christ Church Primary School

S CLUB . . .?

There was a band,
Called S Club 1
Wait, am I sure?
No, there's more.

Or is it,
S Club 2?
I don't think so,
Otherwise they'd live on Looe.

Hang on, hang on,
S Club 3?
I've never seen,
Their family tree.

Somebody said:
S Club 4
But I don't think,
They were very sure.

Maybe it's
S Club 5,
But I'm sure
I've never ever seen them live.

Could it be,
S Club 6?
No, they wouldn't eat
Their weetabix.

I've got it now!
S Club 7,
They're cool and hip,
And their music's pure Heaven.

Grace Glennie-Smith (9)
Christ Church Primary School

THIS IS THE STORY ABOUT ME!

Dear Son,
I know what I've done and I
know how cruel it must seem to everyone
I like to yawn and go to sleep
But when I'm awake
I move swiftly on my feet.
I eat fish
It's my favourite dish.
You know you should have too.
It's full of protein,
And it's got a wonderful taste,
And it's almost as scrumptious as you.
There used to be hardly any of us
but now there's enough to fill a double decker bus.
The reason I ate you
Well it's easy to see
You would grow up to be stronger than me
But I am the Lord and I always shall be.

Amy Lonton-Rawsthorne (100
Christ Church Primary School

BICYCLES

B   icycles, tricycles I like them all.
I   rode mine to the gate,
C   ycles, tricycles, they are great,
Y   ou should like them too.
C   ome with me to the shop,
L   ots of bicycles to buy,
E   veryone in the world,
S   hould have a *bike!*

Holly Denny (9)
Christ Church Primary School

CHINESE NEW YEAR

C hinese New Year, red and gold
H ang all decorations, lanterns and firecrackers
I n dances the dragon and lion, coming down the street
N oise from a drum, you'll hear so loud
E ating all this food that will give good luck
S pecial clothes to wear on the day.
E ating sweets and cakes that give good luck too.

N ew Year is the time we'll get lucky money
E ating all the wrong food will give us bad luck
W ill you see the dragon and lion, will they scare you or not?

Y ou'll see it with a wonderful head, body and tail
E ating cabbage, then throwing it at you
A festival will be shown for everyone to come
R ound goes the year, to the year of the *Snake*.

2001.

Melissa Leung (10)
Christ Church Primary School

CHINESE DRAGONS

Chinese dragons are really cool!
They do what they like and they don't go to school.
Some crazy people think he's really small
But he's twice the size of a swimming pool.
He's 4699 years of age
And should be locked up in a cage.
He is bright and very unfair
He has the longest straggliest hair.
Chinese dragons are really cool!
They do what they like and don't go to school!

Daisy Ursell (9)
Christ Church Primary School

GIRAFFES

Giraffes are tall and
like to play ball.

They don't mind what's
going on behind.

They sniff all around
and lie on the ground.

They hate meat and
lick their feet.

They go to sleep
by the sheep.

They've got long tongues
and big lungs.

They've got little ears
and don't drink beers!

Fatima Rashed (9)
Christ Church Primary School

SPLAT THOSE RATS

Running around the house
Carrying a disease
Running through the house
Looking for some cheese.

Scuttling through the alley
Black and dirty pests,
Scuttling through the alley
Eating food we've left.

So come on, come on
Let's splat those rats,
Come on, come on
Let out the cats!

Michael Stephenson (9)
Christ Church Primary School

S Club 7

S Club 7,
They're my Heaven.
My dream come true,
Even better than meeting all of you.
I wish they were right there,
Staring into my eyes,
Even though it would be a big surprise.
They use such interesting words,
Better than flying with some birds.
Rachel is really pretty,
She comes from the city,
Hannah is really cool,
She probably didn't like school.
Bradley is the man,
No his name isn't Sam.
Paul has an earring,
Jon has a keyring.
Tina has black hair,
Jo's name could be Clare.
S Club 7,
They really are my Heaven.

Caitlin White (9)
Christ Church Primary School

WHEN PIGS FLY

When pigs fly high in the sky
I will know the reason why.

Because it is clear
and it knows how
to jump over the moon
just like the cow.

But as you know
that's make-believe
But of course you know that
So obviously.

Jake McGann (10)
Christ Church Primary School

S CLUB PLANS!

To me S Club are number one
they sing and dance and have lots of fun.
They like to act,
they like to perform,
they like to dress up
nice and warm.
They're hip, cool and trendy,
And have lots of fans and
Visiting my school
I wish I could be one of their plans.
I love them, I love them
I love them so and
I hope to find you do too.

Jessica Lambert (10)
Christ Church Primary School

WHICH YEAR IS IT NOW?

Which year is it?
the
Rat
or
Ox
or it might be the
Tiger
oh no
no way
because
it might be
the
Rabbit
the
Dragon
Snake
Horse
or Sheep
I almost forgot
it
might
be
the
Monkey
or even
Dog or Pig
but no oh no it's the year
of the splendiferous Snake.

William Rich (9)
Christ Church Primary School

THE RATS

Never leave your door ajar
rats come in and they go far
up the stairs or in the hall,
in the cupboard, down the wall
up the curtains, in the lounge
searching, eating, food they scrounge.
In your bedroom, bathroom too
they chew your slippers and your shoe
leaving mess all around
you will hear a scratching sound
it's the noise you dread to hear
they're the ones you know you fear.
Scratching, scraping, biting through
germs and muck they leave their clue.
Rats, rats everywhere
they're in your house and in your hair.
Close your windows
close your doors
sweep up your mess and scrub your floors.
Never let the rats inside
if you do they're sure to hide.
Keep it tidy, keep it clean
or you will know when rats have been.

Rohan Coates (11)
Christ Church Primary School

CRAIG DAVID

I like Craig David's music
I could listen to 'I'm walking away' all day.

I like Craig David's goatee and hair,
But it does require a lot of care.

Do you like dreadlocks too?
But they wouldn't suit you, Craig.

I think Craig David is a good pop star,
he's better by far.

Joe Passafaro (10)
Christ Church Primary School

SNOW! FEAR!

Rushing down the icy hill at incredible speed
You're in desperate need
Feel free like a bird
An avalanche is coming to get you
Crushing everything in its path.
You can feel your fingers tingling
Feet shaking
The avalanche is making a big boulder
You turn, crash smash!
The boulder passes you.
Now that's what you call a dash.
Swoosh, icy snow shattering into pieces
You are zooming
Risking your life
Rolling the dice
Risking your chances.
You're hungry as a bear, cold as ice
But you keep on going,
There is the finish
You bin a win
Losing's not bad, when
You've had a ride like that.

Oliver Gallaugher (10)
Christ Church Primary School

FRUIT HELPS YOUNG AND OLD

(Inspired by the daily newspaper)

Young not old,
Little not tall,
Fruit needed for all,
All you need is a
Little fruit and veggie power,
To keep you healthy and wealthy,
All your life long,
And a little help from apple,
And plum to make you hum.
With cherries and berries,
To make you merry,
And finally some help from
Peas and beans to keep you,
Going right through your teens.

Alice Caird (10)
Christ Church Primary School

RATS!

People think rats are mean,
Horrible and cruel,
Their coats are sleek and shiny,
Their beady eyes are small,
They climb down all your drainpipes,
And underneath your doors,
They run through open windows
And across deserted floors.
But I think rats are lovely,
Elegant and sweet,
They run beneath your floorboards
On their tiny pinkish feet!

Imogen Parkes (9)
Christ Church Primary School

SEVEN HEAVEN

There's a club of seven people,
Three boys, four girls,
All with a cool riddle.
They're a pop group,
Can you guess who it is?

CDs, videos, TV too,
They've conquered all of these,
And you could too.
Just come along and join in the fun,
Think about it and you'll be the one.
Can you guess who it is?

Number one in a million ways,
A band sent from Heaven,
They're all singing and dancing.

It's S Club 7!

Rachel Baker (10)
Christ Church Primary School

CHINESE NEW YEAR

The lion dance is very funny,
Afterwards the children get some money.
Firecrackers are set off at midnight,
To give the monster a big fright.
Fireworks, drums and red decorations
Make up the Chinese New Year celebrations.
Red is for good luck, and gold is for wealth,
In Chinese New Year we don't worry about our health.

Kung Har Fat Choy! (Happy New Year)

Kim Richardson (9)
Christ Church Primary School

RATS

Rats, rats are about.
Do be quiet, do not shout.

They will run away and hide,
If you see one do be kind.

Keep your distance, don't be scared,
Just make sure you're well prepared.

If they run and squeak about
Do remember, do not shout.

Rats have diseases, keep them out
Just to make sure they're not about.

Their coat may be black, their coat may be white,
But don't get too close or they might bite.

Do remember what I said,
Do not put out any bread.

Loretta Holt (10)
Christ Church Primary School

THE DEATH OF A TOMATO

Many years ago lived a tomato.
He was very squeezy, very smooth.
He had loads of pips in him
Tremendously juicy inside and very juicy on the outside.
Do you know how I know this?
Because I ate him!

Arron Hotchkins (10)
Clutton Primary School

THE NIGHT

The darkness is like an enormous black curtain of silk.
Darkness is like the shadow of an unknown shape in the sky.
Dark is like a giant cloud of smoke.
Darkness makes you want to scream your head off.
Darkness makes you want to hide where it can't get you.
Darkness makes owls hoot in silent black sky.
Darkness makes your hair stand on end with the fright of a sound.

Sam Gilbert (9)
Clutton Primary School

DARK

People snoring their heads off.
Black and gloomy.
Foxes howling.
Night is scary.
People go to sleep.
Moles digging.
Stars shining.
Owls hooting.
Badgers whistling.
Night is dark.
Birds asleep.
Rabbits hopping.
Moon is shining
Hedgehogs sneaking.

George Parfitt (8)
Clutton Primary School

THE ALIEN

An immense belly,
Drooped down to ground like a king's cloak,
The belly of an overweight hippo,
Flattening the dew-laden grass.
Its chubby countenance
Was wreathed in a menacing grin.
Its mouth resembled a
Pelican's beak,
Containing millions
Of tiny daggers
Each sharper than an eagle's talon.

They were covered in a gruesome,
Gooey substance,
Falling in a waterfall,
Down to the ground.
Its ten twin legs
Moved and slithered,
Like scaly snakes
Gripping the ground with such ferocity,
They were anacondas by trade.

Its deep turquoise blue eyes
Reflected the sea,
They entranced any watcher!

Its hair dangled down its bumpy back,
A handsome lime green mane.

Its body was covered
In mountain range,
Lumps and bumps.

It slowly started to waddle and stutter down the road,
Like a newborn elephant,
An awesome sight to see!

Matthew Lacey (10)
Clutton Primary School

GRANDPA

Jumping around when he was all jolly,
And one Christmas night he slept on some holly.
When nothing was stirring all through the house,
He stepped on a deep sleeping dormouse.
One dark stormy night,
He went outside with a fright,
When stepping on a banana skin,
And landed in a bin . . .
The next I heard he was in a hospital ward.
(He looked like he was pretty bored).
It gave him an everlasting limp,
Which made him a bit of a wimp.
Later on the poor man died,
And we all said it was with pride.
I'll miss you Grandpa and hope (one day)
That we could go to the park and play.

Keith Marwood (10)
Clutton Primary School

THE PAINTED DOORS

Through the red door I saw my dream team in red kit
winning the world cup.

Through the green door I saw blinding green lights of
the disco at camp.

Through the blue door I saw my private swimming pool
where my friends and me swim.

Through the orange door I saw the blinding sun setting
behind a hill.

Through the purple door I saw the dusk of night
approaching around the town.

Through the yellow door I saw the sun popping out from
behind the hill.

Through the brown door I saw the wood of trees being
cut down to make paper.

Ross Beecroft (10)
Clutton Primary School

MARMALADE THE DEAD HAMSTER

My hamster was there when I needed to talk to someone.
But he didn't understand.
He was adventurous, bold, cute and cuddly
He had escaped three times but we always found him
When he died I tried not to cry
My friend was at my house
I was very upset when he died
I still think of him.
But I know that everything has to die sometime.

Laura Densley (9)
Clutton Primary School

WHAT THE WIND SAID

'Far away is where I've come from' said the wind.
'Guess what I've brought you,'
'What?' I asked.
'Your two grandads alive from the dead
wandering around the church,' the wind said.
'Do you like that?'
'Yes' I said. 'What else?'
'A jungle full of creatures you've never heard of
or seen before,' the wind continued.
'I like the creatures you've never heard of or seen before,' I said.
'What else?'
'A swimming pool with nightingales singing and dancing
around the pool,' the wind went on.
'Do you like that?'
'Yes, I like that,' I said.
'What else?' I asked.
'Your favourite band of S Club 7 singing live on stage!'
'Do you like that?'
'Yes very much' I said.
'What else?' I continued.
'You will sing a duet with Britney Spears,' the wind said,
the wind was getting excited, I could tell.
'I like that!' I replied.
'What else?' I asked.
'A holiday to Italy, and everything free!'
Wow I thought.
'What else?'
'That's not enough?' the wind complained.
'No' I replied, 'I want the song you were singing.'
'Give me that!'

Holly Graham (10)
Clutton Primary School

FIRE

Burning bright and hot,
Sparkling big and red.

Volcanic flames bursting out fast,
Fire balls blasting out fast.

Deadly ashes powerfully boiling,
Sad people running for their lives.

Strong fire melting down anything in its path,
Red, orange, yellow flames burning fast.

Gleaming red and yellow,
The flammable heat from the fire.

Then comes the cold at night,
And the freezing coldness puts it out.

Matthew Sparks (9)
Clutton Primary School

THE DEATH OF A CAT

The cat always purrs,
It never did hurt or harm,
And it always greets people.
Some fat, some thin,
Some big, some small.
It was furry,
It was cuddly,
She was so special to me.
She was so soft and smooth.
I got sad and lonely,
I would never forget that cat!

Joanna Withers (9)
Clutton Primary School

SCAMP, MY DEAD DOG

My black and white fluffy dog
Lived a very happy life.

Jumping up and down
Playing all around.

Barking and running
All day long.

I was sad and lonely when he died
No more jumping for food or running and barking.

I will miss you
But in my heart you will always be.

Victor Higgins (9)
Clutton Primary School

NIGHT-TIME

Darkness makes you shut your eyes,
Darkness makes the moon shine.
Hedgehogs snuffling in the moonlight,
Owls eyes glowing in the night light.
Spiders creeping through your hair,
Stars twinkling in the midnight dark.
Cats eyes lighting up,
In the night badgers crawling.
Foxes hunt for yummy food,
In the night wild animals come.
Darkness is spooky,
People sleeping in their beds so warm.
Headlamps shine in the night light,
Darkness makes people tired.

Vanessa Withey (8)
Clutton Primary School

WHAT THE WIND SAID

'Faraway is where I've come from,' said the wind.
'Guess what I've brought you?'
'What?' I asked curiously.
'I've brought you the golden brown fresh cookies of the
finest bakers' warm oven,' smiled the wind.
'I like that,' I smirked.
'I have also brought to you, the warmth of the golden sun,
upon a pale, red sunset,' sighed the wind.
'What else?' I questioned.
'The blessed life of the just born multicolour parrot,
chirping an echo throughout the calm and still tropical plains,'
dreamed the wind, wearily.
'Beautiful' I thought.
'I have also brought you, the astonishing roar of a football crowd,
who are joyous and happy for their team.'
'Nice one,' I grinned happily.
'Also the trickle of a dynamic stream, in a peaceful, remote forest,'
murmured the wind.
'Brilliant,' I admired it in my thoughts.
'The last is that of great delicacy, the fragile scent of a rose.'
'Perfect.'

Richard Lawlor (11)
Clutton Primary School

THE DEATH OF A POTATO

The potato is round and brown,
Crying when put in water,
He started to cry when his peels dropped in the water.

He was very nice and tasty and juicy,
With a very sparkly brown coat.
He was very easy to peel,
Very tasty when not mouldy and when peeled.

The potato sprouts up when growing,
He was good at hitting bottles,
Very good at playing football,
And suddenly he started growing legs.

After his legs finished growing,
He had something to eat.
But it was poisonous,
Then he started to die.

Christopher Brent 10)
Clutton Primary School

NIGHT-TIME

Night is when the moon shines, as light as you can imagine.
I like it because the stars twinkle in a beautiful creation.
Glowing green catseyes on the road as you pass by,
Hedgehogs shuffle about in the leaves, trying to find a bed.
Torches are lighting up your room, to let you see where to go,
Teatime is over, time to go to bed.
It's time for the foxes and wolves to go hunting.
Mums telling children to go to bed but they won't.
Eating and drinking, my dad does all night,
Awake are the badgers sniffing about for food.
Waking up owls that swoop for their prey,
At night the sky turns dark blue like velvet.
Kicking about are the moles on the grass, looking for a safe
place to stay.
Exploring the open wide world.

Alice Tanner (8)
Clutton Primary School

NIGHT

Night is dark, dull and black,
Moonlight beaming and stars shining.
Owls hooting and badgers waking,
Wolves howling and foxes hunting.
Trees swaying and dogs barking.
Cars beeping and children sleeping.
Lights flashing and cars crashing.
Planes flying and grass swaying.
Cats miaowing and mice squeaking.
Brushing teeth and water running,
Midnight approaching and dawn coming.
Spiders crawling and adults yawning,
Badgers sleeping and children waking.
Night going and morn coming.

Ellen Wickes (8)
Clutton Primary School

NIGHT-TIME

Darkness makes
the moon shine,
the stars twinkle,
and catseyes glow.
Everybody goes to bed before midnight.
Badgers wriggle and shuffle in the dark,
Owls swoop over houses,
Hedgehogs hunt for some food.
Foxes come into your garden.
Creepy-crawlies tiptoe over your bed,
Cars put their headlights on.
Darkness makes you close your eyes,
Headlamps shine so bright at night.

Rachel Bennett (8)
Clutton Primary School

NIGHT

Owls hooting in the trees,
Rabbits munching and drinking,
Dogs barking loud as loud can be.
Stars twinkling, dancing in the moonlight,
Dogs' eyes light and bright.
Cats miaowing as the night goes on,
The moon shining in the sky.
Cats' eyes shining in the light bright sky,
Mice creeping.
Hedgehogs creep over the wet soggy grass,
Cats running all over the ground.

Kelly Hedges (8)
Clutton Primary School

NIGHT

Night is dark,
Night is gloomy,
Owls are hooting,
Foxes are hunting,
I am sleeping in my bed.
I hear a car coming up the drive.
The door is creaking open.
The midnight news is on,
Dogs are barking,
The clouds are dark,
People sleepwalking,
Men are snoring,
It's near morning.
Now it is.

Daniel Raisbeck (8)
Clutton Primary School

NIGHT

Night is dark
But stars and moonshine
Make it look
Like a mythical place
Unknown to mankind.
Catseyes guide cars
Which put on their lights
To light up darkness forth,
Foxes hunt,
And owls swoop down to catch shrews.
Darkness is a home
For night creatures,
Another world,
It sends us
To sleep.
It's like black velvet
Or a dark cloud,
A black duvet
The world of darkness
And moonlight.
Hedgehogs and shrews,
Toads and frogs,
Nightjars and voles
Live in this world,
Where the wild animals rule.

James Tremlett (9)
Clutton Primary School

RED

Red is,
Spicy,
Chilli pepper.
Red is
Colour of a sweater.
Red is
War,
Terror and torn.
Red stands out
Also
Watch out!
Red is
Stop!
When cannon goes
Pop!
Red is courage,
Red is
Rage
Across the writing
Page.
Red is a cherry,
Care for a sherry?
Red is
Blood and
Steam.
Red is a group,
In the team.

May Alexander (9)
Clutton Primary School

NIGHT

Foxes move silently across the field,
Cats' eyes sparkle at night,
Hedgehogs snuffling their way through the bushes,
Stars twinkling in the night.
The moon white as snow in the sky,
Owls hooting in the night.
People fast asleep, dreaming in their beds,
Wind blows silently across the plain,
Leaves rustling in the night,
Bears snoring in their caves.

Catherine Stenner (9)
Clutton Primary School

DARKNESS

Darkness, black velvet shimmering in the sky,
Darkness makes the street lights go on.
Darkness makes the stars gleam in the sky,
Darkness makes the moon glow and gleam.
Darkness is something that gets darker and darker.
Darkness is when you shut your eyes, black is all you see.
Darkness makes catseyes glow yellow.
Darkness comes slowly, slowly.

Victoria Jenkins (9)
Clutton Primary School

DARKNESS

Darkness is a black cloth,
Darkness is a badger.

Darkness makes the stars twinkle,
Darkness is a crafty fox.

Darkness makes the moon shine,
Darkness comes so very soon.

It's as black as a witch's cat
Darkness is a rabbit.

Sophie Howe (8)
Clutton Primary School

NIGHT

Stars twinkle in the night sky,
Cars parked in the drive.

Foxes scrambling across the garden,
Rocks tumbling down rocky mountains.

Dogs barking and frightening foxes,
Frogs swimming in the icy pond.

Owls swooping as quietly as a mouse,
Footballers fooling in the football stadium.

Damien Davies (9)
Clutton Primary School

NIGHT

Badgers running in the night,
Bad dreams giving people a fright.
Owls swooping down from the trees,
Hedgehogs hibernating in the leaves.
Foxes hunting for mice.
Cars bright headlights.
Men coming back from pubs.
People pulling bath plugs.

Steven Taylor (9)
Clutton Primary School

ALIEN

Stomping out of his spaceship,
With a trail of green slime behind him,
Its three eyes in search of food of any kind.

Its giant feet just like a hare's,
Trampling over everything in its path,
While the puffy balls on its body snap, crackle and pop.

It takes rest on a now slime-covered tree,
The control box on its stomach, all shiny and metallic,
But now sparking as it walks.

It moans a high-pitched wail,
Then another even worse than before,
It then fell slowly to the ground,
Leaving behind a deep, low wail as it gradually died.

Ross Dunford (10)
Clutton Primary School

ALIEN!

Leaping like a frog, hunting down its prey of the midnight forest.
Giant fangs digging into flesh.

Snarling, growling, drooling phlegm along the journey.
Its giant claws lashing out at anything that passes.

Its great horns charging at you viciously running you out of track,
Its eyes will glow in the dark seeking you, you can't escape.

Its skin is like wet leather shining in the midnight moon,
bloodless veins popping out of his skin as it gets angrier and angrier . . .

Lily Holloway (11)
Clutton Primary School

THE DEATH OF A FIRE

I'll always remember that fire, dramatic and glowing
in the night!
Blazing the colours orange and red,
Its blistering flames clawing at the air,
Huge glaring eyes spying through the smoke,
Watching out for a predator.

Although not dying yet
It's destroying all the houses
Yellow sparks, like shooting stars.
It's spreading through the land,
Making the sea a pile of ash.
It's getting closer and *closer* and *closer*
People are getting scared.

Only water can put it out,
Here come the floods, the fire engines go.
Their sirens fade into the distance.

The fire let out a sigh of pain
Screech, scowl, scream.
Yell, shout,
Cackle, crackle.
The fire got weaker and weaker,
It goes down and down, until it is only a
a piece of rubble.

Then suddenly *pow* the fire . . . is dead!
I'll always remember that fire.
Dramatic and glowing, burning in the night.

Ruby Cook & Jennifer Stone (9)
Clutton Primary School

SNOW FAIRIES

One very cold and icy night
When the wind was roaring with all its might,
From the heavens came a silver light,
Carried by the snow queen. Oh what a sight!

The queen's lips were the colour of snow,
She was dressed in white lace from top to toe.
Her dark hair was tied in a pearly bow.
With a whisper goodbye she turned to go.

Her little snow fairies up in the sky,
I looked out the window and saw them fly.
Then without warning they started to drop,
Down to the ground without a stop.

There they lay huddled together
To form very snowy weather,
So that when they woke the children had fun
But then alas out came the sun!

Emily May (10)
Colston's Girls' School

THE MIDNIGHT UNICORN

The midnight unicorn swept down from her sky palace.
Her tail and mane made the sky glitter.
Her icy blue eyes set the landscape on fire
And it turned dark blue.

Her hooves drummed on the clouds
As thunder rumbled overhead.
Her tears hit the ground
As the rain pounded down.

Her eyes turned sky-blue,
She slowed down
As one more tear fell
And the sky became light.

Sunrise, the tiger stepped out
Onto the wet dew.
His amber-green eyes shone
As the midnight unicorn returned once again
To her sky palace.

Jade Jetley (11)
Colston's Girls' School

DO YOU RECOGNISE ME?

I have a tail that shows my anger
And a noise that shows my happiness.
My coat looks ruffled when I am scared
And most of the time I have a wet nose.
Thick hairs sprout from my cheeks
Helping balance and a sense of distance.
I am slender
And my coat is smooth, soft.
I have four padded feet but beware!
For they hide dangerous weapons!
I like to snuggle up in someone's lap.
I am a house-dweller,
I enjoy being stroked but not too much.
And I get angry when I am stroked the wrong way.
Keep on the good side of me for I can be
Dangerous!

Lesley-Ann Curtis (10)
Colston's Girls' School

GUESS WHO?

I am big, black and white
One of the world's rarest mammals.
I eat bamboo, leaves and flowers
And I live in thick dense forests.
But you can also find me in zoos.
I have to spend up to twelve hours a day eating,
I am a gentle, placid vegetarian.
I flourish in the summer
And I starve in the winter.
If you're lucky, you'll find me
In the dark forests of China.

Did you guess who? I am a panda!

Rasheena Malik (11)
Colston's Girls' School

THE SNOW

Last night the snow came silently.
Without a warning it came
And filled the world with ice cream sundae,
With whipped meringue and cream.
The trees become still, iced figures,
The bushes like frosted cookies stand,
The houses wear their white furry toppings
And wonder at the change.
The sun with a mischievous smile
Shines upon the snow
Causing it to glitter like diamonds
Before it melts away.

Elly Herbert (12)
Colston's Girls' School

THE SNOW CAT

The frost lay thick upon the ground
When first the Snow Cat came
The sky was bright, a mass of stars
The moon a ball of flame.

No one heard and no one saw
Until it snowed and snowed some more.
This ghostly creature of the night
His green eyes flashing emerald bright.

Stealthily and silently
Step by step he seeks his prey.
Across the snow he creeps
While the dreaming city sleeps.

Where does he come from?
What's the answer?
Where he goes
No one knows!

Daisy Woods (10)
Colston's Girls' School

THE SNOWY UNICORNS

As I snuggled under my covers,
I saw my white skies.
The unicorns came down softly,
Just like snow.
They started to come faster now,
Then suddenly they stopped.
A monkey came from nowhere,
Next thing I saw nothing there.

Sarah Stephenson-White (10)
Colston's Girls' School

ORDERS!

Do this! Do that!
Clean the gerbils feed the cat.

Mow the lawn
Look after Sean.

Plant the flowers
Don't take hours.

Walk the dog
Beware the fog.

Make the coffee
Bring the toffee.

Your room must be tidy
Get rid of that ivy.

Clean the cars
Wash the cars

Get rid of that dough
N O spells *No!*

Alys Fletcher (11)
Colston's Girls' School

THE STORM-BATTLE

The Storm-Cat raged
As I lay in bed that night.
She called on her wolves
And they began to fight.

She called on her eagles
With huge beating wings.
This is the thunder
Of rain that sings.

Then Sunshine the phoenix
Swoops down from the clouds
And with one fierce look
Storm-Cat flees and howls.

Now I won't see the Storm-Cat
Till the next wild night.
Thanks to Sunshine the phoenix
With feathers so bright.

Sarah Vernon (10)
Colston's Girls' School

THE STORM

The thunder rolled in
As the thunder wolf
Trooped out of his lonely den.

He howled,
deafening everyone
down below.
He called out lightning
And out came that huge
golden eagle, squawking.

As it got lighter
A great lion came out
Roared ferociously
And the whole world
Shook.

The eagle and the wolf
howled one last time
And fled into the depths
of the den.

Jane Holmes (10)
Colston's Girls' School

THE WINTER BEAR

As winter approaches
We see the great white bear
Come tumbling down from the mountains
Walking gently over all that is there.

His soft, white fur falls
Covering the ground
Like white diamond brooches
Lying all around.

He's soft to your touch,
But oh so cold to your feet.
He can freeze your nose,
Your hands and toes,
And all that you might meet.

He's a beautiful friend
When you're wrapped up tight.
You may go for a walk
Or sledge if you might.
He's lots of fun, when you are young
But you'd better watch out
If you're past forty-one!

The sad time has come,
For my white friend to leave.
No more can he stay
Now spring's on its way.
I'll see him next year,
But for now he's to leave,
Before he misses the cold winter breeze.

Hannah Vallin (10)
Colston's Girls' School

THE BIG STORM

The Fire-Leopard's eyes glint in the light
As it breathes out flames.
Its tail swishes from side to side.
It loves to play these menacing games.

With a flick of a golden ear
And a blink of his glittering eyes
The Sun-Lion springs right up
And off and away he flies.

He roars at the Fire-Leopard
The leopard roars straight back.
Thunder strikes its vengeance
With an almighty crack.

The leopard retreats as the Sun-Lion calls
The Siamese Cat of the Moon.
At once she appears next to him.
Over the Fire-Leopard she looms.

Together they call the wind up,
It is there with them straight away.
The animals all greet it
Like it's a normal day.

The wind, it blows at the fire
And soon it has all gone out.
The animals cry with happiness,
As they scamper and scuttle about.

When Sun-Lion and Cat of the Moon
Think of the storm and look down,
All they can see of the battle that was
Is a very sad, hot leopard's frown.

Alison Windsor (10)
Colston's Girls' School

UNICORN

Wandering up the lonely mountain
Sparkling stars shimmering above
Dim light pours gently like a water fountain.
You stop.
You look.
A small bird is flying towards you.
No, it can't be a bird.
It's just like a picture from a book.
You watch it getting closer and closer
Bigger and *bigger*
You gasp as it lands beside you.
Its golden wings brush gently against you
Warming your blood like liquor.
Its body is pearly white
Its eyes twinkling blue
Its wings gleam golden:
A unicorn?
It trots up to you
And whispers gently in your ear:
I am your future
I am your past
I have no beginning
I have no end.
Come with me to paradise.

Rosie Garrard (10)
Colston's Girls' School

HOMEWORK

Homework I hate you
You always give me the flu,
I'd rather watch TV
If I could choose what to do.
TV is much more interesting
So much more fun than maths.

Homework oh homework
You really do stink!
I'd much sooner flush you down the sink.
Teachers still think you're the best
But you're the worst to us.
And this morning because of you
I missed the bus.

Sophie Weston (10)
Colston's Girls' School

THE SNOWFLAKE SWAN

I woke up late one night
To find the snow-swan in my sight.
She was flying high in the sky
Her wings beating in her flight.

Una the unicorn has now arisen
To start a new beautiful day.
But in her sights she can spy
The snow-swan fly high up in the sky.

At this she has fire-flames striking sharp.
They beam down at the snow-swan
And she, poor soul, is terrified.

Now her feathers are falling.
They fall softly to the ground
Like little snowdrops.

Una the unicorn's powerful ray
Has melted the snow-swan quite away
And now Una the unicorn of dawn
Returns in triumph to her palace of the morn.

Zuwena Reid-Bailey (11)
Colston's Girls' School

THE STAMPEDE

Gradually the clouds roll threateningly overhead.
The sky turns icy grey
And a low rumble fills the whole world with misery.

They all know that the great stampede is approaching,
The thunder of hooves sounds menacing
Between the blackening clouds.

Suddenly a bolt of blazing, white-hot lightning
Flashes through the wind and rain of the stampede,
Lights up the sky and scorches the world below.

But wait, there's a figure,
silhouetted in the brilliant white light
of the zig-zag bolt.

Slowly the towering clouds part and melt away.
It's the Fire-Dove!
She spreads her great white wings
And begins to display her golden tail feathers
in a ray of glowing sunshine.

With one magical note from her beak
The stampede turns tail reluctantly.
The Thunder-Horses silently mutter, 'We'll be back.'

At last it is dawn again!
The stampede has gone,
And the Fire-Dove's here to stay.

Florence McClelland (11)
Colston's Girls' School

THE STORM

As Moon the peacock spreads her silver tail feathers,
A pack of white wolves hears the call of night
And brings a downside to the weather.
Thundering across the heavy rain clouds,
Their icy breath whirls and spins.
They rouse the sea, a swirling mass of unicorns,
Rushing and rearing,
Manes and tails flying.
The sea is a bubbling rush of angry horses
As the storm rages.

Then as Moon folds in her tail,
The Sun-Tiger steps onto a rain cloud.
It dips beneath him,
But he floats on
Wiping out the storm.
He chases away the ice-wolves of wind,
And the unicorns sink back into the dark depths of the sea.

The Sun-Tiger roars in triumph.
He leaps into the sky where the Sun-Lion joins him,
And they become one.
The Sun-Lion spreads his mane,
And announces a new day.

Hannah White (10)
Colston's Girls' School

WHAT AM I?

Proud and princely, I parade about
Effortlessly elegant.
Almost without a sound I strut and show off
Crowned, curious and cautious.
Occasionally opening my fan-like feathers,
Colours cascade then, cleverly concealed,
Keen to reveal my special kind of splendour.

Charlotte Lonsdale (10)
Colston's Girls' School

THE RAIN

I can flood your streets
And smash your windows.
I can wash you away
Dead or alive.
I'm unpredictable.
I might start
In the middle of the day,
Or the middle of the night.
I get through doors,
I flood your house.
At other times
I'm as calm as can be.
I'm so quiet
You won't notice me.

Kelly Ware (10)
Coniston Primary School

SATS

I wake up early in the morning
And my face is burning with sweat.
I go to school still fearing
There's something bad ahead.

I sit at my desk and wait.
The papers fall against the hard surface.
All I can hear is the ticking of the clock.
I hear the loud voice of my teacher scream.

As we write
I can hear the sounds,
Our brains clicking,
The sweat dripping,
Ink flying,
Pencils snapping,
Clocks ticking.

I look around
All heads down
I inwardly grown

It's now or never!

Kaylee Cullinan (11)
Coniston Primary School

I WOKE UP ON SATs DAY

I woke up on SATs day, suffused with fear.
I knew that my SATs were really too near;
I got up, got dressed and went downstairs,
Suddenly realising
I was full of cares,
My maths for one thing,
My teacher for another;
I was even worried about my mother.
What would she say if I was the hero?
What would she say if I got a zero?

Oooooooh!

Alex Diaper (10)
Coniston Primary School

I AM HATE

I am Hate, a bright blood-red
I feel like spitting fire, angrily burning inside.
I taste like burning hot coals.
I am found in the deepest part of your heart.
I can force you to fight.
I am the *Devil.*
So be afraid . . . be very afraid.

Kristian Barrs (10)
Coniston Primary School

THE RAINBOW

I am full of seven colours,
I shine very brightly,
And glow very lightly.
Whenever you see the sun,
Whenever you see the rain,
Here I come back again.
I can dazzle your eyes,
I can amaze your eyes,
And then I disappear,
Behind the cloud,
Until the sun and rain come out again.

Lorraine Allen (10)
Coniston Primary School

THE TORNADO

I can rip off your roofs and
throw them away.
I can spin dizzyingly for one whole day.
I never surrender or go away.
I wreck your home so
don't mess with me or
Blown away you will be.

Ben Morris (10)
Coniston Primary School

WHAT IS . . . FIRE?

Fire is a wild beast
waiting to get free.

It is black shrouds of evil spirits
hanging in the sky.

It is a firework
waiting to be set off.

It is angry snake's eyes
glistening in the desert sun.

It is the soul of the Devil
burning in hell!

Sammy Martin (9) & Louise Ball (11)
Court-de-Wyck Primary School

WHAT IS . . . EARTH?

The Earth is a blue and green stress ball
being crushed by the hands of man.

It is a multicoloured ball of string
left in an empty, dark drawer.

It is a tangled nest
sitting at the top of a burnt tree.

It is a patch of grass
littered with torn up blue paper.

It is a piece of black coal
burning in the fire of Heaven.

Chloe Headdon (9) & Ashley Johns (10)
Court-de-Wyck Primary School

My Months

January is bright
better than having a fight.

February is cool
better than the pool.

March brings the sun
and some fun.

April doesn't like snow
It blocks the river's flow.

May is okay
It's better than sitting on a bay.

June is a tune
you play with a spoon.

July looks like a pie
better than wearing a tie.

August is a cross
better than my boss.

September is a seed
that grows when you feed.

October is school
I'm sitting on a stool.

November is a time
to drink beer and wine.

December is a day
When we drink and play.

Matt Pilgrim (8)
Golden Valley School

MONTHS

January brings lots of snow
when everything blows.

February brings the rain,
we don't want it to come again.

March brings a little chill,
when children dance round daffodils.

April brings bright days
when children play in the maze.

May brings lots of sheep
that's when everyone leaps.

June brings dry days
when everyone lays.

July brings sunny days
when everyone plays and plays.

August brings blue lakes,
when everyone makes mistakes.

September brings wet days,
when the water wets the hay.

October is a cold time
when everyone eats lime.

November brings weather that's freezing cold,
and everyone's hair turns bold.

December brings lots of presents
and nobody sees any pheasants.

Ben Leaman (8)
Golden Valley School

THE MONTHS

January is the worst,
makes all our balloons burst.

February brings the rain,
Mum thinks that's a right real pain.

March makes me do my art
Lucy watches the horse and cart.

April makes me go to the park,
Then I hear a big big bark.

May sheep have baby lambs,
and somebody wants a new pram.

June brings out the roses
Lucy plants her little posies.

July is the best with the sun
so we think that is really fun.

August brings golden corn,
then a baby lamb is born.

September is very warm
we get up at the crack of dawn.

October can be very chilly
Sometimes we get a bit silly.

November is very dull
It always attracts the seagull.

December Santa comes to my house,
He always frightens away the mouse.

Danielle Horler (8)
Golden Valley School

MONTHS OF THE YEAR

January's when it snows
and on the wall there's a line of crows.

February brings the cold,
when the bouncy ball has been rolled.

March is when it's spring,
and the London church bells ring.

April makes leaves fall off trees,
and everyone gets cold knees.

May brings the spring again
and brothers and sisters are a pain.

June brings the beach,
and teachers teach.

July brings the sun,
and we all have fun.

August brings the corn
when the baby lamb is born.

September is very warm
we wake up at the crack of dawn.

October brings Hallowe'en
when the trees are all still green.

November brings the dull,
when the apple trees are full.

December brings the snow,
when I get a cold toe.

Lucy Smith (8)
Golden Valley School

THE MONTHS

Cool January brings the snow
it also makes our faces glow.

Frosty February brings the rain
watering the flowers again.

Rainy March on its days
little flowers in my gaze.

Cool April by the lake
I just saw a male drake.

Warm May brings the sheep
grazing on the mountain steep.

Hot June brings the sun
also make the children's fun.

Boiling July brings a bird's nest
a male pheasant looking its best.

Warm August with the buzzing bees
the butterflies fluttering on the breeze.

Warm September I saw a pheasant
sighting some rabbit really is pleasant.

Warm October on Hallowe'en night
a light up skeleton gave me a fright.

Chilly November on Guy Fawkes night
watching by torchlight really is bright.

Cold December brings the snow
twirling down to the ground below.

Emily Gingell (8)
Golden Valley School

WINGS

If I had wings
I would scare people
by saying I'm half bat and human

If I had wings
I would touch the moon
and fly back down

If I had wings
I would fly to America
and see lots of wildlife

If I had wings
I would fly out of school
and say yes I'm out

If I had wings
I would fly to Mexico
and get a tan

If I had wings
I would fly to Mars
and see lots of sand swirls.

Luke Jenkins (8)
Golden Valley School

IF I HAD WINGS

If I had wings
I would fly to a different country,
then cross the open seas.

If I had wings
I would fly up to space,
then I would dive back down to the sea.

If I had wings
I would fly to the sun,
then fly to the moon.

If I had wings
I would fly to Newcastle
to see the semi finals.

Ben Tucker (8)
Golden Valley School

WINGS

If I had wings,
I would fly to a different planet,
and even go to Pluto.

If I had wings,
I would fly to a different country,
and have a holiday.

If I had wings,
I would fly to the eclipse
and see the moon.

If I had wings,
I would fly to the river,
and dive in.

If I had wings
I would fly to see Man United,
in the FA Cup Final.

Joshua Bagnall (8)
Golden Valley School

MY VOYAGE TO FRANCE

My journey to France for my holiday
When birds and creatures are gay.

Then we got on the plane
but when we got off it started to rain.

Back in the car a boring sight
wait . . . I'm just beginning to see sunlight.

On the mountains going to Flaine
I wish I was still on the plane.

I'm there now out of the car
Cool, someone just handed me a chocolate bar.

Well that chocolate bar was nice
but when I went skiing I fell over twice.

Tiffany Whitchurch (8)
Golden Valley School

WINGS

If I had wings
I would watch the ants on the earth.

If I had wings
I would fly with the birds
and land in a tree.

If I had wings
I would sit on a house's chimney.

If I had wings
I would have them brighter than a coin.

Jack Newton (9)
Golden Valley School

THE MONTHS OF THE YEAR

January; the first month of the year
All the dads celebrate and drink all the beer.

February; the ground's still rock hard
But anyway no more Christmas cards.

March; brings the world to spring
Out come the bunnies doing hip hop jumping.

April; gets rid of all the snow
and brings back the sea's wild flow.

May; when people have picnics in the park
and bring the dogs for a good bark.

June; most people go on holiday, hooray, hooray
Time for lots of fun and play.

July; when people play sports like cricket
but if you go to a theme park you'll need to buy a ticket.

August; time for the autumn season
it's like that for a reason.

September; brings showers of rain
Use cars as transport and not the train.

October; it's almost wintertime
My favourite month of the year
to make up a Christmas rhyme.

November; it's starting to bring a lot of snow
and it freezes the river's flow.

December; the last month of the year
Like January the dads drink all the beer.

James Smith (8)
Golden Valley School

IF I HAD WINGS

If I had wings I would glide across the sky
feeling the gentle air trickling into my face.

If I had wings I would run in the air
flapping my wings just touching the sea with my feet.

If I had wings I would fly over people's houses
and watch people in their garden watering the spring flowers.

If I had wings I would watch dolphins in the sea
gently doing beautiful dives.

If I had wings I would fly up and up to the clouds
and look down at the world below.

If I had wings I would go to space
and fly gently round all the planets seeing what I could find.

If I had wings I would go to different schools
and circle the playgrounds till the children came out.

If I had wings I would never go to school
and try and find unfound islands instead.

If I had wings I would take people's babies
and give them wings and feed them myself.

If I had wings I would fly around the world
looking for interesting things.

Zoe Lewis (8)
Golden Valley School

THE MONTHS OF THE YEAR

January pushes away the old year
and starts a new year, nice and clear.

February introduces the start of spring,
when all the birds start to sing.

March is the month of Mother's Day,
and so everyone in the world shouts hooray!

April brings pretty flowers,
and all those awful April showers.

May brings lots of little lambs
and not enough water in dams.

June brings lots of pretty roses,
and even more sniffly noses!

July is very cool
but it's even nicer in a swimming pool.

August is the month of corn,
because harvest is about to be born.

October sends a nip in the air
And all the trees start to turn bare.

November sends Guy Fawkes Night
And sometimes the fireworks give little children a fright.

December is the end of the year
but most people have a big Christmas cheer!

Ella Randall (9)
Golden Valley School

IF I HAD WINGS

If I had wings
I would fly like an aeroplane
And glide gently through the sky.

If I had wings
I would land like a bird on the clouds
And see the sun glowing.

If I had wings
I would swerve through the trees
And fly over gardens and fences.

If I had wings
I would land in the treetops
Away from the rain.

If I had wings
I would rest in the trees
When I'm tired.

If I had wings
I would fly around the world
Spying on the people below.

Emma Jarosz (8)
Golden Valley School

IF I HAD WINGS

If I had wings
I would glide through the sky
like a butterfly floating over flowers.

If I had wings
I would swoop over gardens and fences
just like an eagle catching its prey.

If I had wings
I would flutter through the sky
like a bee hunting for pollen.

If I had wings
I would gaze at the monkeys swinging from tree to tree
There are so many things to do
Oh, if only I had wings.

Tamsyn Whitchurch (8)
Golden Valley School

WINGS

If I had wings I would
fly over the ocean and watch
the boats passing by.

If I had wings I would fly
over a mountain and see the view.

If I had wings I would
fly over the desert
and watch the sun set.

If I had wings I would nick
people's ice creams.

If I had wings I would play
on the clouds.

If I had wings I would
fly over the moon.

Gemma Ostler (8)
Golden Valley School

IF I HAD WINGS

If I had wings
I would fly to Hawaii
and watch the sun go down.

If I had wings
I would glide across the sky
until noon.

If I had wings
I would visit all pop stars
and dine with them.

If I had wings
I would go to the moon
and have a picnic with my toys.

If I had wings
I would go to the country
and pick rare flowers.

If I had wings
I would make my own film
and call it 'My Wings'.

If I had wings
I would read books
until I fell asleep.

If I had wings
I would go to the pub
and have a few drinks.

Lucy Cockerton (9)
Golden Valley School

MONTHS

January brings the rain,
and children are in pain.

February brings the cold,
and houses get sold.

March brings the spring
and church bells ring.

April makes the flowers blossom,
and children get a gold bottom.

May brings the sun,
and people are having fun.

June brings the sand
and gel pens get banned

July brings the sun
and we all have a sticky bun.

August brings the beach
and Mum cleans with bleach.

September brings the winter,
and I got a splinter.

October brings my birthday,
and Granny's always pay.

November brings Guy Fawkes Night
and the fireworks give you a fright.

December brings the freezing snow,
and makes houses glow.

Amiee Dowden (9)
Golden Valley School

MY ADVENTURE

When I went on my adventure
I had so much fun.
I went on a special journey,
This is how it begun.

I was sitting on my bed,
Reading my favourite book,
When I herd a weird noise outside,
So I got up to take a look.

There outside was an enormous spaceship,
Hovering in my garden,
And I thought to myself, very angrily,
Excuse me, I beg your pardon.

Then suddenly, as if they had read my mind,
Two aliens came out,
And because I was so shocked,
I started madly running about.

I ran down the stairs,
And flew out the door.
There were many more aliens
Than there were before.

They asked me to step inside their ship,
And skim through the stars.
Ride across the Milky Way,
From the moon to Mars.

Well of course I said yes,
I could hardly say no.
With an opportunity like this,
I really had to go.

So I skipped inside the enormous ship,
And took a spacey seat
Then all the aliens came running in,
and placed a cushion under my feet.

Suddenly with an ear-piercing rumble
We shot into the sky
Higher than the clouds we went,
Oh, ever so high!

Finally, we reached the stars,
What a magnificent sight!
I really couldn't believe,
It almost gave me a fright.

We soared into outer space
Dashing through the stars.
We even landed on the moon,
Also the awesome Mars.

Well, fun can't last forever,
So off we went to my house.
And in I went into my door,
As quiet as a mouse.

Claire Malton (8)
Golden Valley School

VOYAGE POEM

V oyages are so much fun,
O nly when the journey's coming to an end, you feel you've just begun
Y ou are a voyager now,
A lthough you're probably wondering how
G igantic waves hurl you over and then you start getting lower
E ventually the long journey is over.

Hannah Searcy (10)
Golden Valley Primary School

MY TRIP AROUND THE WORLD

On my holiday I'm going to France,
and I'm going to Paris if I have a chance.

Then I'm going to sunny Spain,
to explore the engine of a plane.

Then I'm going to New York city
I can't go shopping, that's a pity.

Then I'm going to India,
to see if it's any windier.

Then I'm going to Japan
to try and find Peter Pan.

Then I'm going to Peru,
to see how the Incas grew.

Then I'm going to the South Pole
to watch an Eskimo dig a hole.

Then I'm going back to England
to go and play in the yellow sand.

Jade Whymark (9)
Golden Valley School

MY VOYAGE

As I started on my deep sea voyage
Across the ocean blue,
In my good ship 'Mensuir Toyage'
I feel like shouting 'Yahoo'.

Very soon a shark came swimming,
Pretty near my boat.
I shot it, quick as a lemming,
Then its body came afloat.

Soon we moored in Rio,
We met an eastern tribe,
'We'll let you go,' said Meo,
'If we get a bribe'.

Hallam Merryweather (10)
Golden Valley Primary School

IF I HAD WINGS

If I had wings
I would touch the golden moon
and swim along in the north wind.

If I had wings
I would fly to Pluto and beyond
and overtake an aeroplane.

If I had wings
I would dive at 3,000 feet
and fly across great blue seas.

If I had wings
I would surf the air
and travel the great wide world.

If I had wings
I would stare at people
who walk down below.

If I had wings
I would dream of
skimming the oceans
and playing catch with the sharks.

Dominique Graeme-Wilson (8)
Golden Valley School

WINGS

If I had wings
I would fly to school
As fast as a speeding bullet.

If I had wings
During the night I would fly away,
Into the starry sky.

If I had wings
I would glide underwater
like a penguin chasing fish.

If I had wings
I would fly like a spitfire
doing loop the loops.

If I had wings
I would lift people up
as if they were a feather.

If I had wings
I would go to the highest treetop
And come back again.

If I had wings
I would go to pet heaven
and see my hamster.

Rhys Matson (8)
Golden Valley School

TRAVELLING ON MY BOAT

My vehicle is a ship,
Sailing the seven seas.

My journey is an orbit
Travelling around in space.

My ship is a deep brown leaf,
Floating on a vast blue silk.

The ocean is a shark,
Eating away at my ship.

Joe Hastings (11)
Golden Valley Primary School

IF I HAD WINGS

If I had wings
I would touch the icy world,
and glide through the frosty air.

If I had wings
I would swim through the cold water,
and dive through a sparkling fountain.

If I had wings
I would fly up to the cheesy moon,
and (fly) back like a bird.

If I had wings
I would dance through the orange flames,
and burn the flames out.

If I had wings
I would fly into the forest,
and meet all of the feathery birds.

If I had wings
I would fly to the sun,
and never get burnt.

If I had wings
I do wish I had wings.

Gemma Howard (8)
Golden Valley School

IF I HAD WINGS

If I had wings
I'd fly up to the blue night sky
and touch the shimmering moon.

If I had wings
I'd land on the clouds
by the penny-coin-sun gleaming in the sky.

If I had wings
I'd breathe the air from clouds
and feel its warmth.

If I had wings
I'd swim with the birds
and fly with the fish.

If I had wings
I'd drift with the snowflakes
and blanket the ground with the snow.

If I had wings
I'd dream a sweet dream
gently falling to the ground.

Sophie Brooks (9)
Golden Valley School

IF I HAD WINGS

If I had wings
I would fly the cold, salt water,
and glide through London.

If I had wings
I would not have to pay to go on holiday
So I could go around the world in eighty days.

If I had wings
I would walk the seven seas
And swim the clouds.

If I had wings
I would fly into space
And land on Mars.

James Minett (9)
Golden Valley School

IF I HAD WINGS

If I had wings
I would swim through ice as cold as knives
and freeze in glittering snow.

If I had wings
I would dance through the red sparks of fire
and burn in the orange sparks of flames.

If I had wings
I would fly up to paradise
and see my reflection on the Earth's seas.

If I had wings
I would melt the freezing frost
to sparkling drops of dew
clinging to the delicate tips of the grass.

If I had wings
I would fly through the rainbow
and see myself in the seven colours of it.

Helana Ryan (9)
Golden Valley School

IF I HAD WINGS

If I had wings
I would glide through the clouds
and pass the bees and butterflies.

If I had wings
I would land on the sun
and eat it like a curry.

If I had wings
I would fly in circles and twist
and fall all the way down.

If I had wings
I would fly all the way to Mum and Dad
and go to my brother Jack as well.

If I had wings
I would build a nest out of twigs
and have a wise owl as well.

Lucy Parry (8)
Golden Valley School

TRAVELLING

I travel in a boat,
I travel in a plane,
I travel in a car
I travel in a train.

I've travelled all around
I've travelled near and far,
I've waved to lots of people
No matter who they are.

Although I like to travel
Sometimes it makes me ill,
To stop myself being sick
I have to take a pill.

Emily Perry (11)
Golden Valley Primary School

IF I HAD WINGS

If I had wings
I would soar high above the clouds,
and eat the moon's cheese.

If I had wings
I would play with my friends,
who live in the blue.

If I had wings
I would go up high
and perch on Everest.

If I had wings
I would play with a butterfly's friend,
and act like a bird.

If I had wings
I would fly away from bullies,
and attack them from above.

If I had wings
I would fly past Pluto,
and discover a tenth planet.

Alexander Child (9)
Golden Valley School

JOURNEY THROUGH THE SEASONS' CELEBRATIONS

The first celebration is the new year
As people watch TV
And drink cans of beer.
The fireworks fly high
The colours fill the sky.

The second celebration is Valentine's Day
People kiss,
While their mothers shout hooray.
People get married
Drive home in a carriage.

The third celebration is for our mothers
She cleans and cooks
And thinks of others.
Her face glows
Happiness she shows.

The fourth celebration is Easter in April
As we find eggs
It gives us a thrill
We eat them all up
'Do you like them?' 'Yup.'

The fifth celebration is Father's Day
All their hard work
And all their money
Every day
Happy Father's Day.

The sixth celebration is Bonfire Night
The scary fireworks
Give me a fright.
I look at their light
It's really bright.

The seventh celebration is Christmas Day
It gives me joy
As we celebrate Jesus' birthday
I know he loves me.
All the way.

Phoebe Pring (9)
Golden Valley School

MY TRAVELLING MIND

Climbing the mountains of my mind
I see the sights and feel the wind
Rushing through my hair
As I twist and turn
Around and around and start my walk again.

As I stand on top of the mountain I take a look down
I watch the birds dive for fish in the sea.

As I watch I find my true inner me!

Ellie Smith (11)
Golden Valley Primary School

IF I HAD WINGS

If I had wings
I'd fly upstairs
so as to not waste time.

If I had wings
I'd walk the silvery waters
and swim the sandy sands.

If I had wings
I'd go to Mars
and have tea with the aliens.

If I had wings
I'd always score
with the basketball.

If I had wings
If I had wings.

Christopher Wall (8)
Golden Valley School

DOLPHIN VOYAGE

Playful, living, bobbing boat,
With its dorsal fins,
Swims the bottlenose dolphin,
Rubber, aqua skin.

The Florida sun on its back
Slicing through the waves,
The dolphin in his travelling,
Warm and sunny days.

When the storm is coming,
Lightning starts to flash,
Courageous dolphin powers on,
Don't wait for it to pass.

He soon rejoins the school,
Basking in his glory,
Others squeak and leap,
As he tells his story.

Robyn Bertram (11)
Golden Valley Primary School

IF I HAD WINGS

If I had wings
I would glide on the wind beneath
and fly to the white fluffy clouds.

If I had wings
I would fly to the boiling sun
and take a huge chunk of it.

If I had wings
I would twirl and flutter up to Heaven.

If I had wings
I would fly to Kenya
and live with the wildlife.

I wish I had wings
I do wish I had wings.

Laurie Turpin (8)
Golden Valley School

WINGS

If I had wings
I would fly amongst the birds
and let them flutter free.

If I had wings
I would soar through the clouds like a jet
and storm through the rain.

If I had wings
I would fly to the rainbow
and swoop down to the treasure.

If I had wings
I would loop the loop like a stunt jet
and have a safe landing.

If I had wings
I would fly to the moon
and shout Hi! To the Earth running through space.

Alex Dorrington (9)
Golden Valley School

CHUGGER

The train winds,
Through the countryside,
Chugger, chugger.

Lunch comes
Everyone is full
Chugger, chugger.

Approaches
The town
Slowing
Chhuuggeerr, chhuuggeerr.

The station comes
Slowing,
Slowing,
Ccccchhhhhhh.

James Bridge (10)
Golden Valley Primary School

IF I HAD WINGS

If I had wings
I would walk on the clouds,
swim in the lake and drink from the sea.

If I had wings
I would run in the desert and
eat a big doughnut and eat it all up.

If I had wings
I would fly up to Heaven and
see my nanny and come back down again.

If I had wings
I would let the leaves flutter
on top of me and fall on the ground.

If I had wings
I would flap my wings up to Heaven
If I had wings, if I had wings.

Sarah Leach (9)
Golden Valley School

MONTHS

Cold January brings out the snow,
makes children's faces light up and glow.

Freezing February brings out the sleet
So lots of people travel to Crete.

Blowy March brings out the rain
Pitter pattering on the windowpane.

April brings the sun out bright
Giving people a wonderful sight.

Windy May brings out the kites
Making children light up bright.

Warm June brings out the sun
Giving children lots of fun.

Boiling July makes babies scream
Making all the grass go green.

Burning August is very hot
Making people laugh a lot.

Shivery September brings out the ice
Making our world look very nice.

Freezing October is very boring
I'd rather be playing football and scoring.

November is a pretty sight
Especially when the sky is bright.

Cold December brings out the deer
Giving people Christmas cheer.

Ben Ricketts (9)
Golden Valley School

AEROPLANE

I'm ready to go,
Passports, luggage, tickets too,
Oh no now I'm in a gigantic queue.

My luggage is in the plane,
Now there's no going back.

Now I'm waiting,
Ready to depart,
I just can't wait for my holiday to start!

Off we go

As I peer out,
What do I see?
Seagulls staring back at me.

It won't be long till I get there,
Sunny Spain is my destination.

Now I can imagine it,
Beaches galore,
Oh what fun I've got in store.

The plane is landing now,
Everyone is excited.

Down, down, down I go,
All the way to the ground.

Aeroplane!

Kathryn Chidzey (10)
Golden Valley School

A VOYAGE TO ME!

Clip-clop, went the carthorse's hooves as we tumbled
Down the dusty, rutted path.
The clothes we carried in wrapped up bundles
On the way from Bath.

Yet another town we pass, Bristol,
And onto Nailsea here we go,
Faster and faster the giant horse ran,
I said 'Bristol and on'
I shouted, 'Stop' but we went faster.

Another city or a town,
Pull on the reigns
And slow right down,
Nailsea 'Stop' I did shout,
As the rattling wheels went out.

I get off the horse's load
Looking for a way to walk.
So many people running, talking.
Going about their daily life
Rushing here, rushing there.

I awoke to hear the sound of a storm,
Crash over here, crash over there,
I strained to hear the worried cries
Of the crew above saving our lives.
The last wave crashed over the bow
The strong rock pierced her belly.

I tried to run
But out I went
Through the gapping hole
Up on a rock I was thrown
By the rough hands that carried me.

Matthew Pugh-Hardy (11)
Golden Valley Primary School

JOURNEY OF A LIFETIME

We've just set off
To look for land
Can't wait to feel my feet beneath the gritty yellow sand
We're sailing on that big, blue, wet ocean
The place where someone left the tap on
Forever filling the wide open space that we call the sea.

Suddenly, the night draws in,
The boat starts to rock,
A wave is approaching.

The morning is here
And all is calm
The wicked storm has long since passed
Everything is peaceful, nothing to fear
What's that I hear the captain call?
Land is near?

We jump off the boat
And land with a splash
We explore the island, the crew and I
There's so much to see, so much to do.

We clamber back onto the minuscule sailing ship
Ready to sail back home to our town, to our home
The journey was magical, a real adventure
I'm so looking forward to the next perfect voyage.
I just can't wait to tell the world of the island we found
It's so amazing I just want to visit it again and again
And again and again and again and again and again and again . . .

Kayley Hatch (11)
Golden Valley Primary School

IF I HAD WINGS

If I had wings
I would let the wind swirl around me
like gravy on a plate.

If I had wings
I would hover under the sun
like a roaring fire above me.

If I had wings
I would glide through a cloud
like a car through fog.

If I had wings
I would pour water over the sun
and make rainbows appear on the Earth.

If I had wings
I would let the world amaze me
with its beauty.

Sophie Mountcastle (9)
Golden Valley School

MOUNTAINS

It was hard to breathe,
But I couldn't leave
I climbed to the top
And saw
Big, fat, white snow
Long, narrow paths
Cold as I was, it turned into an iceberg.

Michael Rickard (11)
Golden Valley Primary School

SUNSET STROLL

The sun overhead gleaming proud in its place,
Helping along with the human race
Memories over the years running through your mind,
Release the worries that you find.
Around the lake fisherman sit,
Resting their conscience, their candles lit
Menacing children, waking the dead,
Scaring the ducks away from their bread
To cross the bridge, pay a toll,
All this happened on my sunset stroll!

James Buckley (10)
Golden Valley Primary School

MOVING

I'm in a car
At the port
Now I'm on a ferry,
With France in sight.
Dock at the port
With plane awaiting
Just in time,
Fly up high
Landing now
At the train station
We get on a train
And puff down the lane.
As I arrive back in Britain
I think to myself
All that transportation.

Nicholas Walker (11)
Golden Valley Primary School

THE DAY THE BOY AND THE DOG WENT FOR A WALK

In the morning, it was cold, wet and cloudy.
I was hungry but I was looking forward to the walk.
The dog and I were both very excited.
The dog barked and jumped at the word 'walkies'.
Then we were off, off exploring with the best dog in the world.
Because I was enjoying the walk, I ignored the cold, the wet and clouds.
It began to rain, but we kept on going.
We reached a stream.
It was bubbling and flowing silently.
There was a bonfire at the other side of the road.
It crackled and glowed in the evening sunlight.
There were some sheep in a field and birds that sang in the trees
                                                    and hedges.
We had got to the destination and so we started the walk back.

Andrew Peet (10)
Golden Valley School

MY VOYAGES

I've travelled far in my car
I like biking much better than hiking
I've been on a plane to see my cousin Wayne
It's really good fun being in a glider looking down at the
                                                    surfboard rider
My one wish is to join F1 and live in Monaco to soak up
                                                    the sun

One sport I hate is to roller skate
I've even been on a cable car
People often say 'How lucky you are.'

Michael Dixon (10)
Golden Valley School

MOUNTAIN JOURNEY

Off to the mountains we go
Like Sir Edmund Hilary long ago
With my gas tanks, backpacks and spikes
And no scooters, skates or bikes.
Off in the distance we can see the snow
Will we make it yes or no?
Halfway up will I accomplish my mission
Or will it still be my ambition.
My gas tanks are running low and
I'm struggling to get over the snow.
Colder and colder I'm getting, it must be the snow,
I need a cup of tea to warm my toes.
I'm higher up the slope now
And I still haven't given up hope.
I'm at the top at last and
If I see the Yeti, I'll run down twice as fast.

Scott Pilgrim (10)
Golden Valley Primary School

THE PLANE JOURNEY

The plane is going down the runway at lightning speed
Then it takes off and it flies like a big majestic bird
Out the window I can see huge marshmallow clouds as
The plane glides through the billowy, blue sky.
The turbulence hits it like a clash of thunder and lightning.
When we are slowly drifting to the ground
                    the people look like tiny matchsticks.

Josh Ralfs (10)
Golden Valley Primary School

Why?

I stood there
shivering when I
looked. I looked down I
said to myself 'A long way
to go.' It's getting colder every second,
I wish I was home in my bed really warm
and safe. I looked up and said 'Twenty more steps
to go and that will make me there '20, 19, 18, 17,
16, 15, 14, beep, beep, beep, beep; beep, beep, beep, beep 'What it's
only a dream, I opened my curtains and looked outside and
I was on a top of a mountain. Why?

Emma Holt (11)
Golden Valley Primary School

Poem

Get in the car
We're travelling far.
Off to the plane.
We're flying to Spain.
Two hours in the air
We are sitting without a care.
We have a meal and a drink
We may have a long blink.
When we get there it will be hot
Let's go and find a sunny spot.
Two weeks here and lots of fun
Sand, sea, beach and sun.

Jasmine Groves (10)
Golden Valley Primary School

OCEAN EXPLORER

I struggled into my wetsuit all clingy
and tight
And heavied on the oxygen tank which certainly
wasn't light
The deep sea flippers looked humungous
on me
But I was ready for my journey to the bottom
of the sea
I somersaulted backwaters off the edge of
the boat
With this gear on I definitely
won't float
As I started my descent the first
thing I saw
Was a million tiny coral fish
(or was it more?)
My underwater camera was snapping
violently
As a sixteen metre octopus passed by me
silently!
Suddenly I realised I was running
out of air
Unfortunately there was no more time
to hang around and stare
I swam up to the surface and climbed
onto the yacht
And peeled off my wetsuit as I was
feeling rather hot.
That night in bed I dreamt of all the things
that I'd seen
If I ever had a chance again I certainly
would be keen.

Julia Turpin (10)
Golden Valley School

THE FAMILY TRIP

When will this journey end?
North or west
The driver knows best
6, 7, 8 or 9
That's the hours of the time.
Passing Gloucester, Cheltenham and Worcester too
Held up at Birmingham in a queue.

Up the M6 driving fast
Speeding cars flashing past.
Colder and colder as we go north
Heaters blowing to clear the frost.
M74 we're nearly there
Getting closer to our family affair.

Through the valleys, hills and glens
Travelling slow to avoid the bends.
Round the corner it suddenly appears
Dalmellington is very near.
Down the moss and past the bing
Look it's Patna we all sing!

Ainsley Ierland (11)
Golden Valley Primary School

VOYAGE TO IRELAND

We boarded the fast ferry at Stranraer
To take us to our destination
Men directed the cars onto the ferry,
And soon we were ready to go.

We found some comfy chairs to sit on
The sea was calm, no waves about
We ate some sandwiches and looked at the view
We looked for land up ahead.

Quite soon we saw the buoys blinking blue and green,
To mark the safe way into the harbour
Soon we were docking at Belfast
And our holiday was about to begin.

Paul McElroy (11)
Golden Valley Primary School

TRAVELLING

Twisting and twirling down the windy street
The sun blazing down, I can barely stand the heat.
Driving past woods with extra tall trees,
Driving past beaches with deep calm seas.
The waves gently rippling onto the sandy shore
The sun sloping higher and dazzling you even more.

Now getting closer to the big city,
Leaving the sea view will be a pity.
Now driving past tall buildings and towers,
No more beautiful meadows of flowers.
Out of the city and moving on,
The deafening noise has gone, gone, gone.

I still hear ringing in my ears,
And I can't wait until it clears.
The excitement is rushing through me,
I can't wait until we can be,
In our hotel or in the street
Everywhere I go I still feel the heat.

By the pool or in the sea,
I know I'll be happy wherever I'll be.

Hazel Campbell (11)
Golden Valley Primary School

POETIC VOYAGES

What shall I travel on today?

I could go gliding in a plane,
Or go whizzing in a train.

I could go right to the top of the bus,
And sit right next to my friend Gus.

I could go riding on my bike,
Or put my boots on and take a hike.

I could travel in the car,
But I sometimes feel sick if I go too far.

I could sail the stormy seas by boat,
Firstly I must put on my coat.

I could take a ride in a lorry,
Although it's very slow if you're in a hurry.

All this travelling it must be said
Has made me tired,
It's time for bed!

Laura Benjamin (10)
Golden Valley Primary School

I WISH...

I'd like to go to Old Trafford
To see my team win so much.
I'd like to see my favourite players,
And shake hands with the manager.

I'll get there by plane,
My favourite way to travel.
With all my friends and family I'll go,
And be back in time for Match Of The Day.

When I get there I'll be playing with the team,
And maybe they'll ask me to be their mascot.
The crowd's cheers I'd remember forever,
It would be a trip I'd never forget!

Max Randall (11)
Golden Valley Primary School

MY POETIC JOURNEY

I'm on a plane
Travelling to Lanzarote.

We're going so slow,
Well it seems that way.

I can't wait until I get there,
So I can see the sights.

We're nearly there,
Only half an hour to go.

It feels as if we're swaying side to side
I think it's just my imagination.

We're starting to land,
We hit the ground in a fast way.

I start to feel sick,
I don't care because we're nearly there!

Yes I'm here,
At last!

That's the end of my poetic journey.

Ashleigh Paterson (10)
Golden Valley Primary School

FLIGHT 47

I'm in my seat, my seat belt's on,
The door is closed, the steps have gone.
The engine starts to growl
My stomach turns on end
As we start down the runway
The plane goes faster,
The engine gets louder,
I can see the wing flaps move
As we get ready to take off into the sky.
When I look through the window,
Everything flashes by.
Faster and faster the wheels turn
The noise of the engine gets louder,
The plane starts to rumble
As the wheels start to leave the ground
Up, up, up higher we go
The houses and cars look like toys now
Until they've disappeared completely
All I can see is a sky of blue with lots of fluffy white clouds
I'm flying.

Gary Freeman (10)
Golden Valley Primary School

A FERRY JOURNEY TO FRANCE

I'm going to France on the ferry
And I am very merry
I'm going up the steps
I'm on!

I'm sailing across the sea
I see tall ships in front of me
I'm so happy to be going to France
I can see the country with a glance.

The sea is rough and the wind is blowing
It is very exciting where we are going
The boat is going up and down
I would rather be somewhere in town.

At last I am going to arrive
I'll get in the car to drive
I am going to the campsite where I am going to stay
And have a very nice holiday.

Catherine Lee (11)
Golden Valley School

THE SEA

As I sail by, I feel like I can fly.
The wind blows in my hair.
Over the sea is a distant land.
The sea is crashing against the boat.
The froth of the water is spreading round.
The waves are angry like a fierce tiger.
And I am standing looking around.

The passengers rush from here to there,
There is an air of excitement.
When will we arrive? What will we see?
Will it be sunny? Will it be rainy?
And I am standing looking around.

The ship is big and full of wonder,
She's gliding softly through the waves.
Not a sound is heard above the crashing waves,
As she gently travels on her way.
And I am standing looking around.

Chris Leeson (10)
Golden Valley School

MY JOURNEY

3, 2, 1, off we go
Will we leave the ground? I do not know
Faster, faster almost there
Nose up, wheels up, what a scare
Climbing, climbing through the air
In my seat I try not to care
Bump, bump, shaken by the plane,
Clouds just like a lion with a mane.
Now I am comfortable
I can just sit back and relax
I can drink my orange juice
And then have a nap.
When I wake up I am almost there
Now I get ready to get off the plane.
Slower, slower, losing height
I try not to look with all my might
Nearer, nearer, here comes the ground,
Rushing to meet us, my heart is starting to pound.
Thump, thump, at last we are down.
The engines are so loud they make me frown
With relief I enter the terminal,
Glad to be back on solid ground
But wait - I have to do it all again to get home!

Chris Thackray (10)
Golden Valley Primary School

THUNDER AND LIGHTNING

Lightning travels so fast in the night,
It's sure to give you a fright,
Lightning is so slow in the day,
It can't even blow you away.

Thunder isn't as fast as lightning,
But it's twice as frightening,
Thunder has a deafening sound,
It pounds so hard on the ground.

Peter Akery (10)
Golden Valley Primary School

MY VOYAGE

I'm flying through the clouds
Watching them go by
I'm watching the world and clouds change shape,
while people down below don't notice.

I see millions of clouds each second
gliding through space and time
ready to take on the sun.

I see a golden ball of fire
driven by flying chariots which circle the Earth.
The golden rays of sunlight hitting me
with all its might.

Finally I see the Earth moving closer to me
I see trees, plants and creatures
People on roads I think.
Suddenly I feel warm and I look up
and see the sun's bright happy face smiling at me.
But the clouds have now disappeared and the
sun is well above me.
The plane has come to a halt.
My voyage has come to an end.

Michaela Johnson (10)
Golden Valley School

IF I HAD WINGS

If I had wings
I would soar through the clouds on a rainy day
and swim in the water within.

If I had wings
I would land on a cliff on sunny days
and pick out fossils.

If I had wings
I would fly into hot volcanoes and out again
before they erupted violently.

If I had wings
I would fly to sunny Africa
and bring home some furry lions.

Ian Maybury (9)
Golden Valley School

TRAVEL

You can travel on a train,
You can travel on a plane,
You can travel high,
You can travel low,
You can travel anywhere you want to go,
You can travel on a bike,
You can travel on a trike,
Now you can travel anytime you like.

Amy Ray (11)
Golden Valley Primary School

IF I WAS A ...

If I was a car I would be going
Ninety down a freeway causing a risk.

If I was a bus I would be dropping
People off and getting people on.

If I was a tractor I would be all day
In a field ploughing the ground.

If I was a boat I would be crossing the
Atlantic Ocean today.

If I was a hovercraft I would be skimming
Across the sea at one hundred miles per hour.

If I was a bicycle I would be going
Along very carefully and steady.

If I was a motorbike I would be zooming
Down the motorway like a zombie.

If I was a lorry I would be very
Slow so I don't cause any accidents.

If I was a scooter I would be moving very
Slow but I don't mind because at least it gets me from A to B.

If I was a train I would be really happy
Because I'm mega fast.

Jamie Ward (11)
Golden Valley Primary School

TRAVELLING TO SCOTLAND

The train is going to Scotland,
The station is fading away.

The train goes clitter, clatter,
while all the people sway.

The train is in a tunnel,
it's like a gloomy cave.

The sun was in the sky,
The fields were passing by.

There in the distance was the Scottish station,
there it was, the big sensation.

Sam Ford (10)
Golden Valley School

A JOURNEY ON A STAR

A poem is a journey,
A journey on a star,
The gateway to your mind,
Just go and step inside.

A poem is a wash,
Of colours, pictures too
Imagine riding on a star,
Wouldn't that be great!

So when you see a shooting star,
Sparkling in the night
Just think about this poem,
And read it out aloud!

Sophie Grainger (10)
Golden Valley Primary School

ARE WE THERE YET?

Sitting in the back of the car
Endlessly rolling over the tar
Are we going the right way?
We've been travelling all day
'Are we there yet?' We all cry.

Sitting in the back of the car
Dad's been driving much too far
Will the road ever end?
Down the cliff we'll descend
'Are we there yet?' We all cry.

Sitting in the back of the car
Our bodies squashed like pickles in a jar
Two thousand, one hundred lorries we've seen
I wonder how many cars there've been
'Are we there yet?' We all cry.

Sitting in the back of the car
We've been travelling so far
Screaming, yelling, playing I Spy
Getting fed up with my little eye
'Are we there yet?' We all cry.

Sitting in this sweaty car
We've been travelling *much* too far
Will our journey ever end?
Down the road and round the bend
'Are we there yet?' We all cry.

Sitting in this moody car
We've been travelling *much* too far
The road signs show us the way
One mile to go
Hip, hip, hooray!

Elizabeth Clarke (10)
Golden Valley Primary School

ON MY VOYAGE I . . .

On my voyage I danced
in France
Slipped
in Greece
Ate
in Turkey

On my journey
I rode an elephant
In Africa
A donkey in Spain
And
A moped in Italy.

My voyage was
fantastico.
Sorry no postcard!

Mark Thompson (10)
Golden Valley School

I'M FLYING TO MIGRATE FOR THE WINTER

I am a bird flying way up high
When I fly, I fly up in the sky.
All of us birds are flying in a line
All of us birds, all feel fine.
I'm flying to migrate for the winter.

Alisha Tinsley-Such (10)
Golden Valley Primary School

THE AMY JOHNSON POEM

The noise of Jason revving up
Amy climbing in
Her goggles down and her scarf wrapped round
She sets off into the unknown
Will she make it? Only God knows.
Will she live or will she die?
I think as she flies up into the sky
I turn away trying not to cry.
Is this really our last goodbye?

Stephanie Tucker (10)
Golden Valley Primary School

THE WHALE OPERA

I'm sitting on a cliff by the sea tonight
Listening to the sounds the whales may sing
The sounds they sing are
Gee-naw,
Gee-naw,
Mmmm-urr,
Mmmm-urr.
I'm sitting on a cliff by the sea tonight
Listening to the sea song, it tells a story,
A whale myth
Which goes like this
Gee-naw,
Gee-naw,
Mmmm-urr,
Mmmm-urr.

Christopher Dibsdall (9)
Grove Junior School

THIS IS THE FARM THAT TONY BUILT

This is the farm
That Tony built.

This is the cow
That lay in the farm
That Tony built.

This is the dog
That chased the cow
That lay in the farm
That Tony built.

This is the bull
That chased the dog
That bit the cow
That lay in the farm
That Tony built.

This is the mystery man
Who shot the bull
Who chased the dog
That bit the cow
Who lay in the farm
That Tony built.

This is Tony
Who caught the mystery man
Who shot the bull
Who chased the dog
Who bit the cow
Who lay in the farm
That Tony built.

John Bown (9)
Grove Junior School

THE HOUSE THAT JADE BUILT

This is the house
That Jade built.

This is the horse
That gallops around outside
The house that Jade built.

This is the rider
That rides the horse
That gallops around outside
The house that Jade built.

This is the dog
That bit the rider
That rides the horse
That gallops around outside
The house that Jade built.

This is the cat
That scratched the dog
That bit the rider
That rides the horse
That gallops around outside
The house that Jade built.

This is the rat
That scared the cat
That scratched the dog
That bit the rider
That rides the horse
That gallops around outside
The house that Jade built.

Grace Cook (10)
Grove Junior School

THIS IS THE BARN

This is the rat
That sneaked in the barn
That Sam built.

This is the cat,
That ate the rat,
That sneaked in the barn,
That Sam built.

This is the horse,
That kicked the cat,
That ate the rat,
That sneaked in the barn,
That Sam built.

This is the bull with a ring on his nose,
That butted the horse,
That kicked the cat,
That ate the rat,
That sneaked in the barn,
That Sam built.

This is the farmer
That owns the bull,
That has a ring on his nose,
That butted the horse,
That kicked the cat,
That ate the rat,
That sneaked in the barn,
That Sam built.

Stephanie Court (9)
Grove Junior School

RAINFOREST MADNESS

This is the forest
That nature built.

This is the tree
That grows in the forest
That nature built.

This is the monkey
That lives in the tree
That grows in the forest
That nature built.

This is the eagle
That ate the monkey
That lives in the tree
That grows in the forest
That nature built.

This is the python with the big forked tongue
That strangled the eagle
That ate the monkey
That lives in the tree
That grew in the forest
That nature built.

This is the hunter with double-barrelled gun
That shot the python with the big forked tongue
That strangled the eagle
That ate the monkey
That lives in the tree
That grew in the forest
That nature built.

Sam Burgess (9)
Grove Junior School

THIS IS THE SCHOOL THAT PAUL BUILT

This is the school
That Paul built.

This is the hall
That fills the school
That Paul built.

This is the broom
That's near the wall
That's in the hall
That fills the school
That Paul built.

This is the doom
That circles the broom
That's near the wall
That's in the hall
That fills the school
That Paul built.

This is the room
Enclosing the doom
That circles the broom
That's near the wall
That's in the hall
That fills the school
That Paul built.

This is the bun
That's in the room
Enclosing the doom
That circles the broom
That's near the wall
That's in the hall
That fills the school
That Paul built.

This is the rum
That's near the bun
That's in the room
Enclosing the doom
That circles the broom
That's near the wall
That's in the hall
That fills the school
That Paul built.

Here's to the teacher
That drank the rum
That's near the bun
That's in the room
Enclosing the doom
That circles the broom
That's near the wall
That's in the hall
That fills the school
That Paul built.

Claire Hodson & Nelisile Dube (9)
Grove Junior School

THIS IS THE FOREST THAT NATURE BUILT

This is the forest
That nature built.

This is the seed
That made the forest
That nature built.

This is the tree
That grew from the seed
That made the forest
That nature built.

This is the fruit all juicy and sweet
That came from the tree
That grew from the seed
That made the forest
That nature built.

This is the monkey all hairy and cute
That ate the fruit all juicy and sweet
That came from the tree
That grew from the seed
That made the forest
That nature built.

This is the leopard who's a brave young brute
That killed the monkey all hairy and cute
That ate the fruit all juicy and sweet
That came from the tree
That grew from the seed
That made the forest
That nature built.

This is the hunter with a smelly old boot
Who shot the leopard who's a brave young brute
That killed the monkey all hairy and cute
That ate the fruit all juicy and sweet
That came from the tree
That grew from the seed
That made the forest
That nature built.

Jenny Tanner (9)
Grove Junior School

POCKET MONEY

P   lenty of choice
O   nly so much to spend
C   ars and toys are too expensive
K   ickable balls are not allowed
E   ven after ages you have very little
T   oo much given to your sister.

M   uch grovelling for more
O   n your knees just for two pence
N   o point in it really
E   ventally you get a reasonable amount
Y   ou are naughty and lose it all.

Andrew McArdle (8)
Grove Junior School

THIS IS THE CAT THAT PAT BOUGHT

This is the cat
That Pat bought.

These are the mice all covered in lice
That played with the cat
That Pat bought.

This is the dog
That scared the cat
That played with the mice all covered in lice
That Pat bought.

This is the horse
That stamped on the dog
That scared the cat
That played with the mice all covered in lice
That Pat bought.

This is the lady
Who rode the horse
That stamped on the dog
That scared the cat
That played with the mice all covered in lice
That Pat bought.

Siobhan Starkey & Ziba Rautenbach (9)
Grove Junior School

THIS IS THE FOREST THAT'S BEING DESTROYED

This is the forest
That's being destroyed.

These are the trees
That grow in the forest
That's being destroyed.

These are the people
That climbed the trees
That grow in the forest
That's being destroyed.

These are the birds
That fly at great ease
That live in the trees
That are being climbed up
That grow in the forest
That's being destroyed.

This is the canopy
With great, big, green leaves
Where birds fly at great ease,
That live in the trees
That are being climbed up,
That grow in the forest
That's being destroyed.

Georgina Bangham (10)
Grove Junior School

THIS IS THE SCHOOL THAT BECKY BUILT

This is the school
That Becky built.

This is the teacher
That works in the school
That Becky built.

This is the student
That helped the teacher
That works in the school
That Becky built.

This is the child
That challenges the student
That helps the teacher
That works in the school
That Becky built.

This is the dog
Which belongs to the child
That challenges the student
That helps the teacher
That works in the school
That Becky built.

This is the cat
That scratches the dog
Who belongs to the child
That challenges the student
That helps the teacher
That works in the school
That Becky built.

This is the rat
That had a disease
Which killed the cat
That scratched the dog
Which belongs to the child
That challenges the student
That helps the teacher
That works in the school
That Becky built.

This is the bird
That ate the rat
Which had a disease
That killed the cat
That scratched the dog
Which belongs to the child
That challenges the student
That helps the teacher
That works in the school
That Becky built.

Becky Thomas (9) & Paul Kington (10)
Grove Junior School

THIS IS THE CELLAR THAT MARK FOUND

This is the cellar
That Mark found.

This is the rat
That lived in the cellar
That Mark found.

This is the cat
That scratched the rat
That lived in the cellar
That Mark found.

This is the fox
That chased the cat
That scratched the rat
That lived in the cellar
That Mark found.

This is the snake
That bit the fox
That chased the cat
That scratched the rat
That lived in the cellar
That Mark found.

This is the deer
That kicked the snake
That bit the fox
That chased the cat
That scratched the rat
That lived in the cellar
That Mark found.

This is the man
That shot the deer
That kicked the snake
That bit the fox
That chased the cat
That scratched the rat
That lived in the cellar
That Mark found.

Lucy Stanford, Emma Cox (9) & Jade Boobyer (10)
Grove Junior School

THE SEA

The whales sing their relaxing song
As the rainbowfish dart around,
And the anemones spring in and out,
And the seagulls hover
Above the deep, blue sea.

The dolphins chat
All day long
And the sharks
Search for food,
Fishes eat the salty plankton
Hoping they won't be dinner.

Eve Hodges (8)
Grove Junior School

THESE ARE THE WINDOWS THAT JACK MADE

These are the windows
That Jack made.

This is the cleaner
That cleans the window
That Jack made.

This is the man who lives in a pan
That pays the cleaner
That cleans the window
That Jack made.

This is the governor
In charge of the man
Who lives in a pan
Who pays the cleaner
Who cleans the window
That Jack made.

This is the leopard
Who's flavoured and feathered
Who ate the governor
In charge of the man
Who lives in a pan
Who pays the cleaner
Who cleans the windows
That Jack made.

This is the vulture
That killed the leopard
All flavoured and feathered
Who ate the governor
In charge of the man
Who lives in a pan
Who pays the cleaner
Who cleans the window
That Jack made.

Sam Burton & Gary Baynton (9)
Grove Junior School

A SHETLAND PONY

A fluffy warm coat
Carrying his cute head high
A cheeky look.

Swishing his black tail
The sun beaming on his back
Munching the green grass.

Anita Hassall (8)
Grove Junior School

THIS IS THE FOREST THAT NATURE BUILT

This is the forest
That nature built.

This is the leaf
That emerged from the forest
That nature built.

This is the yellowy, green caterpillar
Who nibbled the leaf
That emerged from the forest
That nature built.

This is the eagle
Who crunched the caterpillar
Who nibbled the leaf
That emerged from the forest
That nature built.

These are the people
Who stole the eggs
From the eagle
Who crunched the caterpillar
Who nibbled the leaf
That emerged from the forest
That nature built.

This is the rat
That irritated the people
Who stole the eggs
From the eagle
Who crunched the caterpillar
Who nibbled the leaf
That emerged from the forest
That nature built.

This is the monkey
That leaps on the rat
That irritated the people
Who stole the eggs
From the eagle
Who crunched the caterpillar
Who nibbled the leaf
That emerged from the forest
That nature built.

Holly Smith (9)
Grove Junior School

DANIEL'S PETS

Eleven slime slugs, slithering and sliming,
Ten ugly tarantula, crawling and biting,
Nine fat wolves, fat and hungry,
Eight small pot-bellied pigs, all slimy,
Seven bees, buzzing and stinging
Six geese, honking and flying
Five worms, ugly and squiggly
Four pythons, slithering slowly across my duvet,
Three ants, walking around the floor
Two grasshoppers, creaking madly,
One gorilla, wrecking the bedroom.

Daniel Ridge & Christopher Maines (8)
Grove Junior School

THE HOUSE THAT EMILY AND LARA BUILT

This is the mouse
That lived in the house
That we built.

This is the louse
That lived on the mouse
That slept in the house
That we built.

This is the cat
That sleeps on the mat
That ate the louse
That lived on the mouse
That slept in the house
That we built.

This is the dog
That chased the cat
That sleeps on the mat
That ate the louse
That lived on the mouse
That slept in the house
That we built.

This is the horse
That bucked the dog
That chased the cat
That slept on the mat
That ate the louse
That lived on the mouse
That slept in the house
That we built.

This is the girl
Who rode the horse
That bucked the dog
That chased the cat
That slept on the mat
That ate the louse
That lived on the mouse
That sleeps in the house
That we built.

Lara Valseca King & Emily Bowles (9)
Grove Junior School

RACE TRACK

The cars raced along the track on the slippery roads
Coming towards the finish line
All trying to overtake each other
Getting closer
Each second
The cars raced past
The finish line.

Matthew White (9)
Grove Junior School

THIS IS THE HUT THAT BOB BUILT

This is the hut
That Bob built.

This is the egg
That lay in the hut
That Bob built.

This is the snake
That ate the egg
That lay in the hut
That Bob built.

This is the eagle
That scared the snake
That ate the egg
That lay in the hut
That Bob built.

This is the seagull
That pecked the eagle
That scared the snake
That ate the egg
That lay in the hut
That Bob built.

This is the frog
That jumped on the seagull
That pecked the eagle
That scared the snake
That ate the egg
That lay in the hut
That Bob built.

This is the hog
That squished the frog
That jumped on the seagull
That pecked the eagle
That scared the snake
That ate the egg
That lay in the hut
That Bob built.

This is the tiger
That scratched the hog
That squished the frog
That jumped on the seagull
That pecked the eagle
That scared the snake
That ate the egg
That lay in the hut
That bob built.

This is the spider
That webbed the tiger
That scratched the hog
That squished the frog
That jumped on the seagull
That pecked the eagle
That scared the snake
That ate the egg
That lay in the hut
That bob built.

This is the lizard
That licked the spider
That webbed the tiger
That scratched the hog
That squashed the frog
That jumped on the seagull
That pecked the eagle
That scared the snake
That ate the egg
That lay in the hut
That Bob built.

Mark Ingram (9) & Jake Wilding (10)
Grove Junior School

SEA WORLD

Listen to the sea
Dolphins talking loudly
Fishes blowing bubbles
In the lightness of the sea,
Birds crow, flying around
Anemones clutch to rock
In case any danger comes
Fishes hiding behind rocks
So they won't be tea!

Kathy Thomson (9)
Grove Junior School

THIS IS THE CAKE

This is the cake
That Jake baked.

This is the egg
That went in the cake
That Jake baked.

This is the flour
That mixed with egg
That went in the cake
That Jake baked.

This is the fork
That mixed the flour and the egg
That went in the cake
That Jake baked.

This is the jam
That went on the cake
That used the fork
That mixed the flour and egg
That went in the cake
That Jake baked.

This is the cake
That Jake ate
That's filled with the jam
That went on the cake
That used the fork
That mixed the flour and egg
That went in the cake
That Jake baked.

Lawrence Townsend (10) & James Wadsworth (9)
Grove Junior School

SPACE STATION

This is the space station
That NASA built.

This is the launch site
That NASA space station built.

This is the rocket
That was fired up into space
From the launch site
That NASA space station built.

This is Neil Armstrong
Who climbed into the rocket
Which was fired into space
From the launch site
That NASA space station built.

This is the moon
That Neil Armstrong saw
While in the rocket
Which was fired up into space
From the launch site
That NASA space station built.

Joseph Doul (10)
Grove Junior School

VALENTINE

Love is when you like someone,
Love is when you kiss someone,
Love is when you're never gone,
Love is when you're always there.

Love is when you make a good pair,
Love is when you love someone,
Love is when you're in the air,
Love is when you like someone.

Sophie Woods (9)
Overndale School

WORST FIRST, BEST LAST

Breakfast.
I hate eggs,
I hate Coco Pops,
I love bacon,
My brother ties them in knots.

> Lunch.
> I hate pickle,
> And I hate pork
> I love ham,
> I eat it with a fork.

Tea.
I hate coffee,
I hate cake,
I love tea
And I would like a flake.

> Dinner.
> I hate my sprouts
> And I hate my peas,
> I love my turkey
> My mum and dad have teas.

Benjamin Figueiredo (8)
Overndale School

VOYAGE

I asked a fighter pilot
If I could fly the plane Violet
He said 'Yes!'
'Thank you, I will fly my best.'

'Can you give me a test
Flying towards the west?'
'Yes I will!'
Said Bill.

'I want to fly high
Right up into the sky
Have you got a gun
So we can fire at the sun?'

'I love to fly
When I am not shy.
I want to land
So I can play with my band.'

Richard Smith (10)
Overndale School

AUTUMN

In autumn the leaves fall off the trees
Each day there comes flying bees
They are red, yellow, orange, gold, green and brown
All those curled leaves fall down
All the coloured leaves go crinkly
The old people are wrinkly.

Elsbeth Waugh (9)
Overndale School

WHAT'S THAT SOUND?

Could it be a butterfly
Fluttering its wings as it goes by?
Might it be a spider
Riding in a glider?
Or a bumblebee
Going to eat a flea?
What else could it be
Or is it just me?
Should it be a fly
In bed having a lie in?
I don't know what it might have been
Whatever it was
It has not been seen.

James Dimond (10)
Overndale School

MY SISTER

My sister plays all day
With our dog May.

My sister has white skin
My sister lives in a bin.

My sister annoys me all day
I don't know what to say.

I like my sister when she's nice
But she's scared of mice.

She pleases me when she's quiet
But not when she causes a riot.

Cameron Waugh (9)
Overndale School

FIREWORKS

As black as space
Rockets having a race.
As bright as the sun
Like shooting a gun.

The fearsome rockets are loading
Shooting up and exploding
The sparklers are sizzling
Just like whistling.

Catherine wheels are turning
Looks like they're burning
Squids are bouncing
Just like pouncing.

Guy Fawkes is dying
Because he was lying
The bonfire is burning
While children are learning.

Kirsten Gill (9)
Overndale School

AUTUMN

In autumn the leaves fall off the trees.
In autumn we have a lot of breeze.
In autumn the leaves turn yellow and brown.
In autumn the leaves fall to the ground.

We are going out for a ride.
We are having a very good time.
We are going down the lane.
We are picking all the grain.

The wind starts to blow
The lights start to glow
Hallowe'en is ready to come
I am eating a big iced bun.

Charlotte Causon (8)
Overndale School

WORST FIRST, BEST LAST

Breakfast.
I will definitely spit
At bacon because I hate it
I think toast is best
It's tastier than the rest.

Lunch.
Jaffa Cakes I will not eat
Or sandwiches with meat
I like a Classic because it crunches
And crisps for packed lunches.

Tea.
In my mouth I hate raspberries
Or round, big, fat cherries
I like biscuits for my tea
And cake for my tummy.

Dinner.
I don't eat my roast pork
Or spaghetti with a fork
For dinner I like peas
And a small calibrese.

Edward Daniell (9)
Overndale School

THE MAGIC KEY

One hot sunny day
In May
I was playing in the hay.

I found a key
A bright shiny key
I turned round and round
And upside down.

No one knew where the door was
I wondered what was in there
I opened the door
And I saw

A rainbow
I followed it through.
I cut my toe
On a brightly coloured bow.

My mum called me home
I groaned and groaned
All the way home
My mum was so surprised.

When she opened her eyes
And saw the bright shiny key.

Holly Shaw (10)
Overndale School

WHAT'S IN THE STEW?

What's in the stew?
What's in the stew?
I'm going to make this
Just for you.

> I put some carrots in
> And get a bit of sauce
> I get a piece of meat
> From a wild horse.

I put some spiders in
And some gooey leaves
I put some yucky mud in
Yes some wild beasts.

> I rip up paper
> Inside a book
> I go to the coats
> To get a hook.

Lots of pencil cases
With some pencils
What about a light
Or some stencils?

> I get some bricks
> And lots of toy men
> I have a box
> Or what about a pen?

Abigail Britton (8)
Overndale School

WHAT AM I?

I am very hot,
I can spread quickly,
Some say I'm deadly,
I like cold custard and jelly, not!
I like coal, sometimes wood,
Even little children's hoods,
The one thing I hate is water
Because I will die and suffer,
I can't sit on a sofa,
But I wish I could,
Do you know what I am yet?

I am fire.

Hannah Joy (10)
St Anne's CE Primary School

IMAGINE

Imagine if pigs could fly.
Imagine if computers could cry.
Imagine if cats could talk.
Imagine if trees could walk.
Imagine if dogs say moo.
Imagine if I loved you.
Imagine if your face was full of puss.
Imagine if you were a girl but christened Guss.
Imagine if you were me.
Imagine if you drank gallons of tea.
Imagine if the world ended.
Imagine if the globe descended.

Lauren Prince (10)
St Anne's CE Primary School

ANIMALS

I have a dog called Tony,
Who is very, very bony.
I have a rabbit,
With a bad habit.
I have a cat called Matt,
Who lives in a hat.
I have a pony called Mark,
Who lives in a park.
I have a hamster called Bert,
Who lives in dirt.
I have an elephant called Mary,
Who is hairy.
I have a hen called Ben,
Who eats pens.

Matthew Brain (10)
St Anne's CE Primary School

FAMILIES

Do you have a mum
Who is a pain in the bum?
Do you have a dad
Who is very mad?
Do you have a brother
Who acts like his mother?
Do you have a sister
Who sticks to you like a blister?
Do you have a gran
Who likes any man?

Families!

Mark Williams (10)
St Anne's CE Primary School

NIGHT

Stars shine in the midnight skies,
Dogs howl and baby cries,
Dreams whirling around your head,
You're inspired in your bed.

Tuck yourself up nice and snug,
In a big quilted rug
You can't hear anything, not even a peep,
Tossing and turning in your sleep.

The moon is shining bright,
All through the long night.
Later on morn is here,
Birds are singing, they are near.

You stretch, you yawn,
There's dew on the lawn
The sun shines bright,
Until it's out of sight.

Emily Meddings (10)
St Anne's CE Primary School

WHAT AM I?

I am very round,
I live mostly on the ground,
I am black and white,
I get kicked as high as a kite.
What am I?

I have bruises but they don't show,
When I get kicked I'm not low,
My best friend is dirt,
His name is Bert.
What am I?

I hate long thorns
Because they prick me,
Have you guessed yet?
I'm a football.

Daniel Davis (11)
St Anne's CE Primary School

CHRISTMAS DINNER

Christmas meal
No big deal
But when the ice cream comes out
I push and shove
The people I love
To get there first.

I run to the kitchen
Grab the ice cream
And squirt on
Chocolate sauce!

But the peas
Yuck!
I throw them at my sister
And at my brother
By then I get carried away
And throw them at my mother.

Carrots and sprouts
I spit them out
And they land
In a horrible mess on the floor.

Apart from all this
My meal is bliss.

Tamasyn Russell (11)
St Anne's CE Primary School

TIGERS

Tigers with their bright black stripes
Moving gracefully at night
Looking, watching, quite a sight
All the tigers upright.

Trying not to make a sound
In case the prey can hear their paws on the ground
If the prey can hear oh dear, oh dear
They'll run up a tree or anything near.

Chase, chase, the big race
Will the tigers win or lose?
Scampers, stops
The prey tries to go faster
Tiger's the master
Catches them every day.

Tigers catch
Prey loses the match
Perhaps they'll win someday soon
But right now the tigers have a feast
Under the bright, light moon.

Hayley Entwistle (10)
St Anne's CE Primary School

THE HORSE

The horse gallops out of sight
Into the night
The horse gleams,
The stars beam.

The horse glistens,
The horse listens.
The horse is faster,
The horse is a master.

The horse plays,
The horse stays.
The horse gleams,
The stars beam.

The horse is kind,
The horse has a mind.
The horse is wild,
The horse is like a child.

Amie Strawford (10)
St Anne's CE Primary School

THE THING

It's white and fluffy
And looks like a teddy bear.
It has sharp teeth and claws
To scratch and bite.
It has black eyes and lips
And a small, black sniffing nose.
It has floppy, white ears that flap in the wind.
Its tail is fluffy from going side to side
Have you guessed what it is yet?
Well here are a few more clues,
It chases cars until called,
It seems always hungry too.
This friendly fellow just loves to play the day away.
Its little pink tongue is always licking away
And of course he's mine,
Still haven't guessed?
Well here's just one more clue,
It chases the cat and goes woof, woof,
Yes, of course, it's *Muffin.*

Felicity Braund (11)
St Anne's CE Primary School

GORILLAS

In the jungle gorillas live
Eating fruit and leaves
Animals roam across the land
Frightened by the sound.

Enormous hands
With humongous fingers
And feet the size of plates
Big sharp teeth
And tall broad bodies
Completely covered with hair.

Jamie Oliver (11)
St Anne's CE Primary School

SPACE ADVENTURE

Aliens, aliens everywhere,
Aliens, aliens with no hair.

Aliens, aliens flying around,
Aliens, aliens making no sound.

Aliens, aliens from planet Zog,
Aliens, aliens who sit on a log.

Aliens, aliens who sit and sigh
Aliens, aliens who say 'Goodbye.'

Karl George (10)
St Anne's CE Primary School

ANIMALS

Have you ever had a cat
And he didn't come back?

Have you ever had a fish
Which lived in a dish?

Have you ever had a bat
That lived in a hat?

Have you ever had a fox
That lived in a box?

Have you ever had a boar
That joined in a war?

Have you ever had a mole
And he lived in a bowl?

Have you ever seen a horse
That dressed up like Morse?

Have you ever had a whale
Which went a little pale?

Have you ever had a tiger
Who likes drinking cider?

Have you ever had a snake
Which lived in a lake?

Scott Tegg (10)
St Anne's CE Primary School

SOPHIE

My name is Sophie
I'm very, very small
But some people say I'm rather tall,
I have a loving family,
That care for me,
And one named Lauren, do you see?

I sit on her lap every morning
But when she comes down she is yawning
I have a cat flap that's the window to the world,
And when they go away I get very bored.

I'm not allowed upstairs,
But if I go up I get rather scared,
They give me a dirty look,
Why do I dare?

If I got lost they would care,
Especially Lauren,
I'd make her cry.

Lauren Carr (9)
St Mary's CE Primary School

TOILETS

There's a lovely school called St Mary's
Where the toilets are not that nice,
The adults don't seem to bother
They've never looked to be precise.

There's a lovely school called St Mary's
Where the toilets are not that nice,
They're rotten, yucky and horrid
In fact they're crawling with lice.

There's a lovely school called St Mary's
Where the toilets are not that nice,
Nobody seems to like them
If they were worse we'd be invaded by mice!

Jessica Thomas (9)
St Mary's CE Primary School

MUM'S DAY IN BED

Mum's staying in bed today
Yes she's staying in bed
How is she going to get us organised?
She's sending the zoo instead!

The black-tailed prairie dogs
Are staying in my room
To help me have some fun today
With the brand new vacuum.

Christopher can have the monkeys
(Well he is one himself really!)
They make his room a great big mess
But he is still quite cheery.

Amanda has the elephants
To help her with her homework
After all elephants never forget
Even if it's phone work.

If Mum would shift she'd have the penguins
And they would waddle about
Making the biggest mess of her room
Until we heard her shout!

Heather Nicholls (9)
St Mary's CE Primary School

Ten Things I Found In Mr Jones' Room

Stickers for perfect people,
Pens for writing 'Good',
Computer for playing games on,
A book of really bad jokes,
A box of matches for lighting the candles,
Magazines for his spare time,
Secret stash of chocolate for eating at break,
A spinning chair for, well, spinning,
Loads of books on being a good headteacher,
And a portable television for watching football matches!

Rachel Drew (9)
St Mary's CE Primary School

Inside Mrs Humphrey's Handbag

Inside Mrs Humphrey's handbag you will find . . .
A loud speaker for yelling,
A stick for hitting people,
Some water for calming down,
Some ageing cream to make her look younger,
A manual for her computer,
A calculator for doing the mental sums
And some lipstick for special occasions.

Alex Slim (9)
St Mary's CE Primary School

Snowdrops

Snowdrops burst with love for the forgotten
Only to die and return to their graves
Another year passes back they come
To comfort the dead once more.

Up above the towering trees
The church tower stretches taller
Higher, higher up it goes
As the wind whispers through its windows.

Harriet Dudbridge (9)
St Mary's CE Primary School

INSIDE MY BACK PACK

Inside my back pack you will find . . .
A piece of paper which is lines,
A lunchbox with food inside,
A Harry Potter book, quick look inside,
A PE kit that's a week old,
Look that's my homework there's a fold,
A small pocket for my secrets not to be told.

Andrew Wilson (9)
St Mary's CE Primary School

MR LION

Mr Lion, Mr Lion,
You're so soft and squidgy.
Mr Lion, Mr Lion,
I take him everywhere with me.
Mr Lion, Mr Lion,
With your mustard yellow suit.
Mr Lion, Mr Lion,
Oh you're just so cute!

Francesca Murden (9)
St Mary's CE Primary School

THE BOMB

There once lived a boy called Tom
He wanted to set off a bomb
His mum came along
Said that's very wrong
Bang! That was the end of young Tom.

Christopher Rae (9)
St Mary's CE Primary School

THE GHOST

There once was a ghost called Nick,
All the food in the house he would lick,
Marmalade and ham,
And strawberry jam,
Until at the end he felt sick.

Louis Surdyk (10)
St Mary's CE Primary School

THE ZOO

Monkeys in the cage,
Filled up with rage,
Rattling and clattering the bars.
Lions are sleeping,
Giraffes are eating,
Children are running around!

Tom Carter (9)
St Mary's CE Primary School

THE WORLD

The waters were grey
And then they turned blue
And then there was land
And then there was you.

Then animals came
Two each were the same
And the world was created by God.

Nathaniel Jacquemain (9)
St Mary's CE Primary School

A LIMERICK

There was an old man with a stick
Which all the time he would lick,
It tasted like cheese
Bananas and peas
That silly old man with a stick.

Amber Crookes (9)
St Mary's CE Primary School

TWO MEN

There once were two lucky men
Who lived in a comfortable den
It flooded to the top
Their ears went pop
What an end for the men in the den!

Jamie Bradford (9)
St Mary's CE Primary School

ELKE

There's a teddy that I know
That I like to show
To all of my friends
His name is Elke.
His fur is chocolate brown,
His antlers are muddy brown,
He has no fleas,
But he likes munching green leaves.
His eyes are chocolate, muddy brown
He has white on his ears
And white on his feet
And toes.
I love him
And he loves me.

Sheryl Thompson (9)
St Mary's CE Primary School

WHAT ARE THEY?

From Fanta's (Class 5's pet fish) point of view!

When the bell goes they run to class
On the way, the cloakroom they pass,
They start their day and in a way
I'm still on my holiday.
On comes lunchtime and they've worked hard
When it's Christmas they get a card,
At the end of school at five past three
They go home and start their tea.

Paul Timms (9)
St Mary's CE Primary School

THE GIRLS AND BOYS AT ST MARY'S

There's a lovely school called St Mary's
Where the girls practice dances and play,
The boys fight about the girls' noisiness
But whenever we have visitors they always say:

'Aren't those girls and boys really lovely,
Look at those girls with ribbons in their hair
Can you see those boys having wheelbarrow races?
I hope they take great care.'

'Oh the teachers here are wonderful,
Fandabydozy some might say.'
But to ask the teachers to describe the children
All they would say is:

'Oh, they're OK!'

Sophie Kethro (9)
St Mary's CE Primary School

I'M DEVE

I'm Deve, I'm three weeks old
I'm a hot water bottle case,
I need two hands to hold,
I'm a devil with devil red hair,
My owner will cry if I'm not there.
I hold a black fork to protect us,
I get taken everywhere even on the bus
So I'm a devil with devil red hair
My owner will cry if I'm not there.

Lisa Marie Read (9)
St Mary's CE Primary School

THE TIGHT ROPE WALKER

It's
The tight
Rope walker
Wow!
He's
So
Brave, cool
He's the best, I'm going to be just
Like him
Come on

I hope	he gets
To the	other
Side.	Wow!
He's the	best man

He's almost there, come on, nearly, yeah! He got to the

other
side
he
is
the
coolest.

Nick Miller (9)
St Mary's CE Primary School

FIRE AT MY FEET

The fire at my feet is the evil of the world.
The flames at my toes are what burn the royal pearl.

The sparks in my eyes are what bring down trees and bush.
The blaze at my knees is what helps the waves to push.

Rachael Ware (9)
St Mary's CE Primary School

RIDDLE

Green light-flasher,
Red light-basher,
Screen-saver,
Noise-maker,
Mouse-mover,
Word-remover,
Keyboard-letter,
Typing-better,
Picture-printer,
Idea-hinter,
Disk-spinner,
Neatness-winner,
Desk-sitter,
I'm no quitter

What am I?

Ryan Hale (9)
St Mary's CE Primary School

BUDSY BEAR

Budsy Bear you're my favourite bud
We make each other happy with a great big hug
Your black beady eyes that match the dark
And when we're asleep we're nice and snug.

Budsy, Budsy, you're furry, soft and squidgy
With your sky blue clothes and your mud brown fur
You make me happy when I'm feeling blue
We'll be best buds just me and you.

Lydia Smith (9)
St Mary's CE Primary School

FRANCESCA

There's a grand little lass called Francesca
She's chirpy plus so merry and bright,
She's been my best friend for ages,
Had lots of fun, sleeps over night.

She's always been there when I need her
And never a minute away
I'm sure I shall never forget her
And hope it's best friends we shall stay.

I've known that she's always loved pizza
And burgers and thin stringy chips,
She's also enjoyed sausage pies
Loves Tizer and takes it in sips.

She loves to read and write
And also loves to sleep
She doesn't snore or nothing
She does not give a peep.

We'll stay best buds no matter what
No one will ever change that
We are so inseparable
We always like a chat.

She's never there when I phone
And always up and out,
So when I get fed up
I've got to give her a shout.

Laura Ford (9)
St Mary's CE Primary School

I LOVE BUBBLES

I love bubbles,
They sparkle in the bath,
They sparkle in the sun.
They're more than that, they say,
But I don't care.
Because I'm special in every way.
And so is everyone else.

The bubbles say that I get away, but from what?
They say well, us, you hate us.
I don't hate you, in a surprising way.
But you don't think we're special
I do, but I don't know in what way.

I'll see you tomorrow, I'll softly say
See you, but we don't want to go
If you do I will see you tomorrow, well OK, but you better promise
OK I promise. Goodnight and sleep tight
Bye the bubbles said in a sad way.

At first I felt bad,
To see the bubbles sad.
So I made them a card,
To cheer them up.
It was bright blue with bubbles I made, stuck on to it.
It said inside,
Dear bubbles
You're so kind and sweet, please don't cry.

They were glad to see it in the morning,
And they said thank you.
We played all day until dawn I said bye,
And they cried.
So I went home sad and never saw them again.

Amy Wheeler (10)
Silverhill School

COMPLAINTS ABOUT MY HOUSE

It's a house with a kitchen,
A house with a door,
All the rest is spooky, very, very, spooky.
It grumbles at night-time
It's a house on the river,
Bats on the ceiling, mice on the floor.

I sometimes think
There's a monster under my house.
My house is spooky, very, very spooky.
It wakes me at night-time
With grumbles and groans, clattering and banging
And hopefully that's probably all.

Oh yes! Please don't forget
My house is spooky very, very spooky.

Joshua Reason (9)
Silverhill School

SNOW IS . . .

Snow is a falling shower of frozen flowers floating softly down.

Snow is a land of beauty, untouched by man.

Snow is a white feathery landscape far as the eye can spy.

Snow is a crisp snowman or snowball.

Snow is a land of slush and mush.

Snow is a beauty gone forever.

Joseph Tregear (10)
Silverhill School

SELECTING YOUR DOG

A bit too big,
A little too small,
Too fuzzy for me,
Too fat to crawl.

Before you wrap it tight
And crate it home
Behold its appetite
And room to roam.

A sloppy yap, a barking slur,
Puppy eyes to be let free,
A him? A her? An unmarked fur,
Let's pout to see its pedigree
The perfect pet quest,
Which pup for me is best?

Russell Avenin (8)
Silverhill School

THE FUNKY BEAT

Far from the sound of the pounding feet
Came dinosaurs with the funky beat
There were Trannies, Sauruses and Triceratops too,
All rushing along to Christopher's zoo.
All of a sudden there's a mighty roar,
And along came a lion and look,
One more.
We weren't frightened as the animals came,
Because they all were friendly and most were tame
So it's out into fields, no cages here,
'Cause one thing we hate is an animal's tear.

Christopher Brown (8)
Silverhill School

THE DREAM

When I get snuggled up in bed
The dreams start filling my head.

I dream I'm a sailor sailing the seven seas
Or even a wild animal prancing with glee.

I dream I'm an alien roaming the moon
And a shark knowing he'll be fed soon.

But sometimes I have bad dreams, sad dreams
I dream I'm in a plane crash
Or that I've caught a deadly red rash.

But in the morning when the cock has crowed
I cannot remember the dreams that have shown me
The terrible scenes of good and bad,
Which has made me happy or sad.

Francesca Norris (9)
Silverhill School

THE WITCH

Sitting on her broom flying in the air
Galloping out into the mist
Muttering spells as she flies
Causing havoc in the town
Waving her hand high in the air
Landing her broom wherever she wants
She creeps up behind you
Puff you're a frog.

Gareth Knowles (10)
Silverhill School

SPACESHIP

If I were an astronaut,
I would have the best view in the world
But from where I'm standing
I have to settle with a dot moving across the sky.

She is a great space traveller
And that's probably what gives her the name
'The Traveller'.

She is the colour of mud with gold lining
And they say dead people live there!

She has a mast and sails and little portholes and metal bars
Around the edges.

If only I could be there
On the spaceship.

Gregory Sturge (9)
Silverhill School

THE FOREST

As we walk through the forest
The sun shines in and makes patterns on the floor.

As we walk through the forest
You can hear the rippling of the water.

As we walk through the forest
The birds rustle their feathers and twitter.

As we walk through the forest
We can hear the lambs in the field.

Edward Bourns (10)
Silverhill School

LIAPHANT

Lies beneath the undergrowth
As the sewer swells
Goes up and down, all around
But never goes over ground.

His name is Mr Liaphant
He loves the smelly sewers
He drinks out of a big pipe
What leads to Boston Square.

When he got hungry
He went down the line
He saw a burnt up motor car
With the engine small and grey
He slammed it and crushed
And gulped it down and away.

Liaphant was a big creature
He found it hard to breathe
Until a little mouse
Had a little scream
He ran around in circles
Until he lost some weight
He never got fat again.
That old Liaphant.

Joshua Oware (9)
Silverhill School

DREAM SHIP

Floating through clouds of cold ice cream
The wooden ship has gossamer sails
The purple sky twinkles and sings
Close your eyes, rest your eyes,
Whisper goodnight, silent goodnight.

Passing birds twitter pretty words,
And the stars in the sky shimmer like sapphires
The songs of dreams passes around,
Dream ship, dream ship, glide and slide,
Dream ship, dream ship, deliver sweet dreams.

Jessica Milsom (11)
Silverhill School

THE STORM

The glistening moon shining so bright
Like thick, white chalk
It shines over the city like a magic carpet
The thunder sounds like an ear-piercing scream
The lightning cracks through the sky
I know that this is the
Storm, storm, storm.

Up on the beach the sea is slashing
Against the jaggardy cliff face,
As it beats against the sand,
The palm trees blow back,
No one in sight,
I know that this is the
Storm, storm, storm.

My eyes slowly open as I lie in bed,
I remember the
Storm, storm, storm
As I swiftly draw the curtains,
Nothing is now there.

Nazia Mulla (10)
Silverhill School

INDIAN EARTHQUAKE

Old and young crying,
Wailing for their loved ones
Who they will see no more.

People struggling in vain
To save thousands out of the rubble
Which used to be their homes.

It's a strange thought
That in less than one minute
A civilised world could be turned into living hell.

Thousands dead and thousands still missing.
What has come to this once beautiful country?

In no time at all millions of lives
Have been wrecked and ruined.
For some there doesn't seem much point in living.

People trying to live in ramshackle little huts
Made out of rescued parts of people's homes.

These people have nothing except
Themselves and the clothes they're in.

It makes you think how lucky we really are
We have clothes, food and a roof over our head.

Catherine Perry (10)
Silverhill School

ONE SNOWY MORNING

The windows as white as snow
The wind blow freezing cold at my face
The grass was whiter than a polar bear
Snow sprinkled down from the sky.

A thick, white blanket on the grass
Without marks or traces
I stopped and turned around to see
My footprints in the snow.

Nicole Crompton (9)
Silverhill School

A WINTER'S MORNING

I went out one winter's morning
Out to a bitter cold day
The snowdrops were falling off a branch
On that cold and awful day
The water glistened on the web
The snow started falling like tiny drops of rain.

The wind howled like howling ghosts
I tightened my coat as the wind blew
I felt Jack Frost tickling me
As he pulled me back to the tree
Luckily I wriggled out
Then I was free.

Then a squirrel was scurrying
Across the frosty ground
Then I heard a voice
Coming across the ground
Then I heard her shout 'Tom'
Luckily it was my mum.

She said 'Come, come, come
Go straight to bed
When you get home.'
'Oh no!'

Jack Maddox (9)
Silverhill School

IN MY WORLD

Lakes lie in hidden boundaries
As clear as the finest fresh crystals
Rippled with ravenous ruby red
Tinted with succulent sapphire blue
With elegant emeralds twinkling in the sparkling sunlight.

Graceful birds flutter their frolicful fanned feathers
Sweetly singing their harmonious songs
Bearing beautiful feathers touched by the rainbow!
Tinted with reds and oranges, yellows and greens
Not bothered about the tedious world around them.

Exotic animals roam the lands, all kinds roam freely
Dancing dolphins, silver-fanned fish and waltzing whales too!
Bouncing dogs, cute little kittens and bashful bunnies few
They live in peace and harmony with no fear to fill their minds
All animals may live in peace and share their precious kinds
No man to kill, no dog to hunt
Peace and harmony may rule their exotic lives.

Monstrous marshmallow-filled mountains, hide the
                              chocolate-coated streams
The dips in the mountains are hot, bubbly, creamy caramel lagoons
Crystally-coated in sweet sugar!
Tall trees bear toffee apples and lollipops!
Blossom of marzipan, with fairy babies inside
Bold bushes, bearing sweet sugar balls and chocolate elves
                                    provide the chocolate!

In my world fun is a law
No wars to feed and provide poverty
The old can grow old (if they want to) they have happy lives also!
You never die, only if you're in pain
My rules, would be no animal cruelty, poaching or poverty!
My world is beautiful and warfare cannot be seen
For the only thing that can be seen is peace, peace, peace!

Joanna Norris (10)
Silverhill School

POLITICS

Politicians are a pain, they're rich enough as it is,
They're putting up the petrol prices,
We'll never live with this.

There's crisis and shortages all because of the ministers
If they're not careful they'll turn the globe into a gas cylinder.

I suppose they do a little bit now and again
Like raising the odd appeal
But even hearing the name Tony Blair
Now makes me feel ill.

He's going to get elected next time,
Or so he thinks
If you ask me he's straight out of the question
Same with almost everyone I expect.

Oliver Shepherd (11)
Silverhill School

THE DREAM

As soon as I go to sleep
I imagine a pirate ship
Gliding through space like a bird,
With wretched pirates searching for gold,
And their hostage is Mary Poppins.
Meteors pass as swift as swans.
The rings of Saturn turn and turn,
They never burn.
The sun bubbles like boiling water
Boiling in a pan.
While Mrs Spare as I dared was sitting on the moon.
Venus was like a tennis ball circling round and round.
Uranus could talk.
He bawled out he was the best at everything.
Alisha was riding stars around the moon.
I could see the clouds circling the Earth.
Suddenly meteors crashed on the Earth!
And all that was left were crumbs.

And that's the end of my dream.

Charlotte Macleod (9)
Silverhill School

THE CAT'S DAY

As the cat's prowling through the grass,
It sees a butterfly fluttering through the soft air,
The cat slowly creeps closer and closer,
Suddenly the paws crash together like cymbals in a orchestra
The first catch of the day.

A mouse scurries across the path,
The cat pounces on it,
Then pushes to make it run as fast as it can,
But it can't and soon dies,
The second catch of the day.

Samantha McCouig (9)
Silverhill School

SPACE WONDER

I look up in the sky at night
And wonder who's up there.
The stars they twinkle shiny and bright
As up in the sky I stare.

Is there a Martian living on Mars
Or a Venetian living on Venus?
Do you think the Martians drive around in cars?
If they did, it would be tremendous.

I'm sure they have spaceships in which they can travel
Many a light year in space.
Perhaps one day they will land on the gravel
Near my house and we'll come face to face.

Till then I'll keep dreaming of how they'll look when I see them.
Will they be green with big ears or like ET?
They may look like monsters when they come, who knows when
Or perhaps they will look just like me.

Joshua Goddard (9)
Silverhill School

THE ANGRY TEACHER

I sat upon my chair, feet trembling in my shoes
'Jack.'
'Yes, Miss.'
'What have you done now?'
The angry teacher shouted
Slowly, hatred-full she approached me
Her eyes glaring at this moment
Fire shooting from her nose
My conscience was saying 'Tell the truth.'
I looked up, that raging figure stood before me
The tables turned, instead I told a lie
Though my conscience shall haunt me till I die.

Edward Moyse (11)
Silverhill School

POETIC VOYAGE

I sail in my ship on the breath of the wind
Gliding on my candyfloss clouds,
They change from white to pink
And seem to link into the deep blue sea sky
As I go further into space I seem to find a special place
Which produces fluffy cotton wool words
That float past on bright shining stars
That are not yellow or gold but green with purple spots,
And a sun and a moon which are not one but lots
Imagine all the colours,
Imagine all the shapes,
I've only been there once but I think it's great!

Amber Thomas (10)
Silverhill School

THE SECRET

Today's the day
I am going to the picnic
Through the lush, lush grass
And next to the sweet, sweet water
From the pure, pure waterfall.
But lying there next to it all
Is me.
And only I alone
Will ever know that secret patch
Of land down
Through the lush, lush grass
And next to the sweet, sweet water
From the pure, pure waterfall.
Every time I visit I feel so much younger
I will grow older
And the secret will die with me.

Thomas Drury (11)
Silverhill School

IF I WAS A RABBIT

If I was a rabbit I would love to run around
I hate to be picked up by the belly from the ground
I hate to be stuck in a cage all day
But I love the feel of the stroking on my back
I hate going to the vet and having injections
I would love to run around in the open
I hate being run over by cars
I hate it.

Robbie Williamson (8)
Silverhill School

THE LIONS

They lie there all day long
Given their daily food
But never knowing why,
They're not set free to roam.

They stare as the watchers go by
With their flashy cameras
Knowing they're there to be watched
But never knowing why
They can't be with their friends.

They try to break away
But are thwarted
By the deadly darts.

Samuel Hobbs (10)
Silverhill School

THE SHELL

And then I pressed the shell
Close to my ear,
And listened well.

And straight away like a bell,
Came low and clear
The slow, sad murmur of fair distant seas.

Whipped by an icy breeze
Upon a shore
Wind-swept and desolate.

It was a sunless sand that never bore
The footprints of a man,
Nor felt the weight.

Charlotte Lacey (9)
Silverhill School

MY PET

My pet, is the best pet
The best pet you can get,
He slides up to his frisbee
His back legs lift as he halts.

My pet, is the best pet,
The best pet you can get,
He is man's best friend,
Especially mine.

My pet, is the best pet
The best pet you can get,
He is all my world,
Because he is
The best dog in the world.

Alastair Bradley (10)
Silverhill School

MORNING COMES

Morning comes
With my brother shouting.

Morning comes
With taps running.

Morning comes
With my dad's car revving.

Morning comes
With me dressing.

Morning comes
With me just listening.

Ben Saunders (10)
Silverhill School

THE DREAM

I close my eyes
Off I go to my
Dreamland

I see aliens
Floating
Around
And
Around.

Octopuses dancing
In the sea then . . .
I started
Dancing.

Then I saw flowers
Some were laughing
But some were
Crying.

*Oh! It was only
In my dreamland.*

**Alisha Braley (9)
Silverhill School**

NAPOLEON'S BATH TUB

Napoleon had a bath tub
It was his pride and joy
Large enough for Napoleon
And his yellow ducky toy.

The walls were made of marble
The taps were made of gold
Even the soap, tied on a rope
Was priceless, so I'm told.

After months campaigning
He'd come home for a soak
With ducky boy and loofah
And several small boats.

He'd sigh a deep contented sigh
And say 'Why do I roam
When I have such a lovely bath
Waiting for me at home?'

Fergus Woods (11)
Silverhill School

OCTOBER THOUGHTS

I remember, I remember,
My birthday in October,
All the presents I had
But soon it was all over.

I remember, I remember,
The day when Granny died,
And the sad time it brought,
How sad we were.

I remember, I remember,
When baby George was born,
The crying and the feeding,
The happy time it was.

I remember, I remember,
When Grandad was seventy,
All the cards like me,
He was getting old he was.

Angharad Conner (11)
Silverhill School

CLOUDS

What is a cloud like?
Can you jump on it or lie on it,
How does it float in the air?
When I was young I always used to think
It was one giant bubble that got stuck way up there.
Can you go inside it or even control it
So you could go wherever you would like to go?
You could travel around the countryside in it
And nobody would ever know.
Can you touch it, can you feel it, is it really there?
The misty shapes of animals that are running through the air
I sometimes wondered whether it was the same bubbles from your bath
That got on your nose and always made you laugh.

Louisa Paling (11)
Silverhill School

THE SEA

The sea is so blue on a sunny day
So calm, so still, allowing people to stay
To float, to swim, to dive, to play
But when a hurricane comes this way
The sea so grey - a foaming bed
So noisy, so fierce, the fisherman's dread.
Clinging to their lines, to keep afloat
Praying for the safety of their boat
Then, my favourite time a gentle breeze
When you can sail on the peaceful seas.
The bow of the boat breaks the waves
And the sun glimmers through the haze.

Andrew Matson (11)
Silverhill School

IS THERE LIFE ON MARS?

Is there life on Mars?
If so, what do they eat and why do they fly?
Are they green?
No! They're blue.
And why
Do they ride the Milky Way and do they spy?
And why
If there is life on Mars, why can't we see it?
Is it human, do they stand, can they sit?
Maybe they're just like us
Driving cars and taking the bus.
Spending money, having a Maccy-D,
Going to school, maths and PE.
Or maybe not human at all
Big bulging eyes and wobbly legs with rocks
And craters for their beds.
I'm not sure what happens at all
Does the sun shine, does the rain fall?
Do they have winter, summer or spring?
Do they have Christmas carols to sing?
Mars is a mystery to you and me,
Spinning in the universe, fast and free.
The astronauts fly in rockets to see,
If the occupants of Mars could live with you and me
One day we will know, if we could live on Mars.
I hope it's soon before I get old and I can tell the kids,
We're off, the house is sold.

Alexandra Hucker (10)
Silverhill School

SNOW

I love snow
When winter comes I wait for snow
The snow feels crisp beneath my toes.
I love snow!
When I walk through the snow
I see animals footprints, humans prints, trails, trails and more trails.
I love snow!
Adults walk out the door and get splatted with snowballs -
Not very happy!
I love snow!
Snowmen with carrots on their noses with buttons for his toesies
Thick scarves, tall hats and twigs
For his arms all in all
I love snow!

Stephanie Averis (11)
Silverhill School

THE RED FOX

He shoots his prey with a giant leap
And eats them in the most disgusting way.
He darts through the forest like a bullet
Till he catches his prey.
All animals try to avoid him but
Some do not manage
Stalks, watches,
Then makes a move.
He stumbles on the ridged edge of a cliff
Falls through the air,
Screaming for help he lands on his back,
And that is the end of fox.

Oliver Cook (10)
Silverhill School

MY PUPPY

My puppy had an adventure,
My puppy thinks he's a pirate
He thinks he's on a ship
But he's only at home
Having a sleep.
He grunts through the night
Dreaming of buried treasure
There's not a moment to lose
He sounds his horn
To alarm his crew.
We're setting sail next light
And when the tide is right
Get ready to polish the cannon
And to load the food
Raise the flag
And stand by to raise the anchor
We'll sail through the night
The sun was shining
And the sea was calm
But later that night
The rain poured down
The wind howled
The ship swayed from side to side
For two days and two nights
All I could think about
Where was the treasure?
Are we any closer?
Or is my dream coming to an end?
Please, please
Let me sleep
For I am in search of treasure.

Tom Wilson (9)
Silverhill School

THE MOAN

I'm always sent to my room when I'm naughty,
There's nothing to do in my bedroom.
I want to go to the mall,
But I can't.

I want, I want,
Some Game Boy games.
I really need some Game Boy games.
I've only got one and I need some more
My batteries are wearing out
And the sound is really poor.

It's not very good on my Game Boy
I haven't got enough games
I haven't got a computer.
It's boring in my bedroom
There's nothing I can do.

Why do I have to be sent here
For everything I do.
It's just not fair,
I don't get my way,
I'm always in the wrong.
Perhaps next time,
Maybe next time,
I might just behave,
Just maybe.

Aaron Thomas (8)
Silverhill School

THE HAUNTED HOUSE

It's evil and dark behind that door
Someone rich could be in there
Or even someone poor.
The path was slimy and green
The door looked frightening and mean.

Inside is quiet and dusty
Everything was old and rusty.

My bones feel cold.

I shiver and quake
With every step I take.

What will I find behind the door
Ghosts and goblins and so much more!

Natasha Martin (10)
Silverhill School

A CAT'S LIFE

I hate people who touch my carpet.
I hate people who touch my beautiful claws.
I hate people who touch my coat of armour.
I hate people who like dogs.
The worst thing is I can't stand it anymore
But the worst thing is being locked out in the
Rain.

Stuart Tayler (8)
Silverhill School

MY JUNGLE BEDROOM

When I go through the door,
I hear the lions roar,
I wonder what there is,
The cats purr and the snakes hiss
Some lions lie on the sandy soil
The snakes glide across the ground, just like oil,
The tigers creep in among the plants that shine,
And the pleasure's all mine,
To walk through the jungle at night.

A creepy cave comes into sight,
A bright thing in it, a little light,
A sleeping dragon, when he snores, smoke rises from his nose,
I dash to the door,
A baby dragon comes out of the floor,
Shortly followed by his friend,
Then they run around a bend,
The sleeping dragon is only one of the lot,
And I am trampled down,
By that herd of dragons in dressing gowns,
After I am squashed flat,
I run out of all that.

I walk to the water to take a peek at the fish,
And I fall in,
It's like falling in a water-filled dustbin,
And now all that time has passed, I can see my bed at last,
I jump in and go to sleep,
An hour has gone past, I am woken up by sheep,
I think my jungle is still there,
But it's my farm, a boring morning,
I hear my family yawning.

Andrew Moyse (9)
Silverhill School

MY BEDROOM

When I play in my bedroom
I see a jungle, I wander to the big mean green jungle
I wander through the whispering grass,
Then I heard a fierce roar, the sound grew louder.

So I ran like a speedy cheetah across the sandy land,
Then I saw a sabre-tooth tiger with a fierce look,
He was a few metres away from me, his attitude grew very fierce,
Then I crouched under a rock,
The tiger ran away in the blazing hot jungle.

Then a pirate ship appeared,
The ground changed to sea,
The pirate ship fell to the sea,
I was on a log, some cannon balls shot at me,
So I dived in the freezing cold water,
I found a chest
I opened it,
Then I got sucked into my modern bedroom.

Then I said thank goodness for that.

Matthew Allen (8)
Silverhill School

THE ELEPHANT

The elephant twists and crushes as it is twisting houses up,
Tossing them into piles as they mount up and up.

Then the whirlwind cuts out as the elephant
Twists its way out of the town, to blow another place.

Louis Blackwell (10)
Silverhill School

THE WIND

The wind whistles past.
The wind fanned through my hands.
The wind wafts through my hair.
The wind puffed in my eyes.
The wind blasted through my ears.

Nick Frost (9)
Silverhill High School

BLACK HORSE

Black horse,
Magic horse,
Carry me away,
Across the Atlantic,
Ice cracking,
Ice splitting,
Animals floating away.

Casey Beardmore (8)
Stockwood Green Primary School

BROWN DEER

Brown deer,
Magic deer,
Carry me away,
To the Arctic day,
And see the polar bears play.

Brown deer,
Magic deer,
Carry me away,
To the sandy bay,
And watch the people play.

Brown deer,
Magic deer,
Carry me away,
To see the Grinch
Grow one inch.

Mitchell Carroll (7)
Stockwood Green Primary School

MAGIC BIRD

Magic bird,
Multicoloured bird,
Carry me away,
To America,
To see MGM,
To go in the big ball,
It's going to be very fun when
We go down the waterfall.

Magic bird,
Multicoloured bird,
Carry me away
To America
So I can go to the seaside,
With the big, big wave
And the thunder slide.

Magic bird,
Multicoloured bird,
Carry me away,
To Lego Land
To play with the learning cats,
And go on the water slide,
We went on the merry-go-round.

Donna Jacobson (8)
Stockwood Green Primary School

PAPI'S PIG

My papi had a pig called Gertie,
She rolled in the mud and got very dirty.
She liked to run round the field a lot,
Quite fast for a great big Gloucester Spot.

I've been for a ride on the back of Gertie,
And when I got off, my clothes were all dusty.
Mummy took some photos of me
With Gertie sniffing both my knees.

I've been on a bus, a bike and a car,
On those you can travel both near and far.
I've even been for a tractor ride,
Sat next to Papi bursting with pride.

But the best way to travel, I think I've found
Is not on a pony or a shaggy great hound,
But sitting on tightly, on the back of a pig,
As it runs round the field with a jiggedy jig.

Hayley Clements (8)
Stockwood Green Primary School

GOLD CARPET

Gold carpet,
Magic carpet,
Carry me away,
Find a place to stay,
Find a beautiful palace,
And eat nuts today.

Gold carpet,
Magic carpet,
Carry me away,
Find a place to stay,
Go to Mexico,
And say 'Ole'.

Louise Baker (8)
Stockwood Green Primary School

THE DAY I FELL DOWN THE TOILET

On a voyage.

The day I fell down the toilet
Was when I was on an ark,
I went out in the sea
And almost got eaten by a shark.

When I hit a storm
I was drifted away,
I was half a mile up coast
When I found a beach bay.

Then I saw the voyage
The big white ship,
Coming to dock
At the hickory whip.

Jamie Bridgeman (8)
Stockwood Green Primary School

THE JOURNEY

I'm on my way for a long day's trip
To a place where I like to skip
I hope the sun shines very bright,
And the stars stay out all night.

The place I would like to be the most
Is lying by the sunny coast
I count the waves ten by ten
And dive in and out of them.

Lauren Curtis (9)
Stockwood Green Primary School

PEAS, POTATO AND PIE

Waiter! Waiter!
Tell the chef I want this in my pie . . .
The Indian desert with a sprig of China
My peas . . . shall be meteorites
Crashing down to Earth
And the potatoes shall be rocks off sandy shores
My gravy, the sea
Oh and my drink is the . . .
Atlantic with icebergs floating
And for dessert yes I blurt
I want Mars spinning round the moon
Now that's all, that is all
Yes I know it's absurd
But don't speak a word.

Collette Raine (10)
The Meadows Primary School

WINNIE THE POOH

Winnie The Pooh, oh, Winnie The Pooh,
He is as fat as a pig.
Winnie The Pooh, oh, Winnie The Pooh,
You are a cute kitten.
Winnie The Pooh, oh, Winnie The Pooh,
You are just like a Trojan horse.
Winnie The Pooh, oh, Winnie The Pooh,
Your jacket is red as beetroot.
Winnie The Pooh, oh, Winnie The Pooh,
Your nose is always with you.
Winnie The Pooh, oh, Winnie The Pooh,
Just say you are so sweet.
Winnie The Pooh, oh, Winnie The Pooh,
You have lots of friends just like Roo.
Winnie The Pooh, oh, Winnie The Pooh,
Your best friend is Piglet but sometimes Roo.
Winnie The Pooh, oh, Winnie The Pooh,
Your friend is Christopher Robin too.
Winnie The Pooh, oh, Winnie The Pooh,
Just come to me.
Winnie The Pooh, oh, Winnie The Pooh,
Can you cuddle me?
Winnie The Pooh, oh, Winnie The Pooh,
Your stomach is full of honey.
Winnie The Pooh, oh, Winnie The Pooh,
You have a friend and she is a bunny.
Winnie The Pooh, oh, Winnie The Pooh,
I will always be with you.

Katie Riseley (10)
The Meadows Primary School

MY PLEASURE PLACE

The sea it waves like galloping white horses,
Through its sandy tide race courses.

Though the wind whirls round and round,
Nobody is heard, no one hears a sound.

The sun in the sky shines royal and grand,
While people relax on the warm, golden sand.

The wind opens its mouth and blows and sighs,
And whistles around the clear blue skies.

Women lay on the sand and wait,
For the sun to break out of the cloudy gate.

Shells are scattered all around the sea bed,
The warmth is the boss, the leader, the head.

The sun burns up and shines its rays,
Through the nights and through the days.

I just wait for the warmth to bounce off me
In this pleasure place of sun, sand and sea.

Danielle Gay (10)
The Meadows Primary School

MUSIC VS FOOTIE

Music vs Footie is here today
The conductor blew his whistle around
The crowd is off and so are the teams
Andante has got the ball with no sound.

Crescendo is up the right wing
Can Diminuendo get the ball off him
Crescendo blows the ball to his team mate Con-spirito
Con-spirito by Forte got him down by his skin.

Footie's goalie can he save the shot
Nooo! Great try but a great shot from Con-spirito
A rebound from Mezza Forte
It goes in!
Wasn't allowed? What?

All music team complained
The conductor went on
Won't get you anywhere
But they still shone.

Luke Gordon Coles (10)
The Meadows Primary School

BACK TO SCHOOL

Back to school, back to school,
To prove to Daddy that I'm not a fool
With my head held high and my shoes tied tight
I hope I don't get in a fight.

Back to school, back to school,
To prove to Daddy that I'm not a fool
My Mumma makes a fuss because I catch the school bus,
I hope the school dinners are not made of mush.

Back to school, back to school,
To prove to Daddy that I'm not a fool
Every Friday we have a test, but all I can do is try my best
Yea I got an 'A'.

Back to school, back to school,
To prove to Daddy that I'm not a fool
It makes me cry but there is something that I can't deny
I will go there till the day I die.

Jamie Case (11)
The Meadows Primary School

QUESTIONS

For my sister, Katie.

'Polar bear, oh, polar bear,
How is your coat so white?'
'Katie dear, oh, Katie dear,
You are very polite!'

'Bunny kin, oh, bunny kin,
How do you run so fast?'
'Katie dear, oh, Katie dear,
My running does not last!'

'Mooey cow, oh, mooey cow,
How do you moo all day?'
'Katie dear, oh, Katie dear,
Well, I don't like to neigh!'

'Perky pig, oh, perky pig,
How do you eat a lot?'
'Katie dear, oh, Katie dear,
I eat all the food I've got!'

Joanne Riseley (10)
The Meadows Primary School

FOOTBALL MAD!

Football!
Long hard training
Running laps round the gym
Heading and shooting at the goal
Hard work!

Football!
Getting muddy
Hard, sharp sliding tackles
Penalty disasters, oh no
Muddy!

Football!
Be the captain
Shouting at your teammates
I hate getting dropped from the team
Watch out!

Football!
I have new boots
They are clean and shiny
I really like my new Nike boots
Wicked!

Liam Osborne (11)
The Meadows Primary School

HORSES

Galloping round wild and free
Jumping over fallen down trees
Eating green grass and golden hay
Appaloosa and dappled grey.

They were used in the wars,
And walked across the soggy moors
Dressed in armour nice and smart
Made up of every strong part.

Peaceful, calm and lovely creatures,
Gorgeous faces and lovely features
Eating, sleeping is all they do,
You love them and they'll love you!

Galloping round wild and free
Jumping over fallen down trees
Eating green grass and golden hay
Appaloosa and dappled grey.

Madeleine Wride (11)
The Meadows Primary School

BROOKE THE PUPPY

Brooke the puppy
Is small and dark brown
She tumbles and stumbles
And bounces around.

Brooke the puppy
Is sometimes quite sleepy
But otherwise she is
Energetic but creepy.

Brooke the puppy
Likes chewing the mail
And barking at visitors
And chasing her tail.

Brooke the puppy
Can get in small places
She wriggles and wiggles
Puts smiles on our faces.

Brooke the puppy
Has wonderful owners
They're happy and joyful
Not moaners and groaners.

Brooke the puppy
Is a right little creature
She's sneaky and mischievous
But no one can teach her.

Brooke the puppy
Has black, floppy ears
And I hope she will live
For plenty more years.

Kirsty Hooper (11)
The Meadows Primary School

HOLIDAY FUN!

I'm in the sunny Cornwall
Croyde to be exact
Hills are all around me
The landscape is filled with summer, the rays of sunshine shine on it.

I'm staying in a big tent
With my sleeping bag outstretched,
The beach is right beside me
And that's where I like best.

The sand has tiny granules each with a tiny golden glint
The shells are found all over the sand
But none can compare with the sea
Its blue waves and white froth make it look like a monster
          with a moustache.

I run down to the sand with my brothers
Across the long stretch of sand
I reach my destiny
The sea!

On goes my swimming suit
Off goes my shoes
Grab my board
And off I go!

I jump in the sea
The stones scratch my feet
The seaweed slaps my leg
The water makes me shiver as I go deeper.

The waves are getting bigger now
I grab my board as I see a big one coming
I'm picked up from the ground, I'm flying
I land flat on the sand and run back to the sea to do it again!

Zoe Richards (10)
The Meadows Primary School

SPORTS

Hockey, swimming, football, netball
Some people play them all
Doing sports is great
For people that want to lose weight.

I love hockey
But people are sometimes cocky
Pass the ball
And I'll score a goal.

I love swimming
It's not like singing
When you do butterfly
Try not to poke anybody in the eye.

I love football
I love kicking balls
Tapping, scoring, kicking hard
Trying not to kick people as if they're card.

I love netball
I like passing ball
Got to catch, got to pass, shoot now
But how?

Of course there are others
For your mothers
You can do any sports
Most of them in courts.

Amber Smith (11)
The Meadows Primary School

SEALS

A seal is like a bird,
Swift, elegant and graceful,
And is the first class master,
They love to eat
They love to be friendly,
The seals are masters
Masters of all the sea.

The seal is like King Arthur
Stout, cheerful and friendly,
Loves to play games,
Loves to be free,
The seals are wonders
Wonders of all the sea.

Seals are like wolves,
Hunting down the crabs,
Scavenging the dead fish
Consuming everything in its path,
The seals are scavengers,
Scavengers in the sea.

The seal is endangered,
Endangered as can be,
Is being hunted down one by one,
As far as the eye can see,
The seal is endangered,
Endangered from you and me.

Joshua Pullan (10)
The Meadows Primary School

SPORT

Football
I have new boots
I really like my boots
Shouting and scoring at the goal
Wicked!

Netball
With ball don't move
Shooting hoops at the park
I get them in most of the time
Goodie!

Singing
Have a good voice
Sing to the audience
Make some dance moves with the song
Groovy!

Cricket
Bowl the round ball,
Hitting it for a six
There are lots of kinds of back strokes
Hit it!

Joe Harrison (10)
The Meadows Primary School

MY BROTHER

There was a boy called Peter
For Peter was his name
Who was like most brothers
And drove his mum insane.

He enjoys his cup of telly
With his annoying attitude
And as for my granny
She finds it always rude.

He can be very nasty
His claws, he can well, scratch
And his feet they can't half kick
And is not afraid to snatch.

And at the age of seven
He's in bad boys' heaven
With a heart full of gold
He's as bad as hell he's told.

Yes I know he's annoying
But there's bound to be another
Yes I know he's horrid
But remember he's my brother.

Alice Dobie (10)
The Meadows Primary School

SEALS

Here is the story of a seal's life
With nice cute puppies and a lovely wife
Many seals are just grey and only see them in May
Seals still are nice in seal sanctuaries
But the seals don't like it when it's manky
Seals have a lot of skill,
And catch fish for their meals
In the sanctuary there is a seal called Scooby,
He claps his flippers and is never moody.
Seals are hunter haters, but are big fish daters.
Seals have blubber, six and a half centimetres wide,
But can still take people on his back for a ride
When seals are asleep, their nose is automatic
And I find loads of ornaments of seals in the attic
The seals have a habitat, the ocean and the sea,
But seals greatest fan is forever and always me.

Jamie Bunker (10)
The Meadows Primary School

SCHOOL RAP

School, school it goes to my head,
Every night when I go to bed,
I worry about the slightest things,
But I won't forget the joy it brings,
I always get frustrated during a test,
But all I can do is try my best,
My teacher I think is really fun,
If you ask me she's number one.

Daniel Langdon (10)
The Meadows Primary School

MY BROTHER

He's a puddle-maker,
A food-taker
He likes hiding,
And he likes riding,
He likes quad biking,
He acts like a Viking,
He likes looking at the stars
And eating Mars bars.
He collects Beanies,
And he loves the Tweenies,
My birthday's in September
My brother's is in November
Yippee!

Toby Long (10)
The Meadows Primary School

MARS

Mars is red and yellow with cream,
Unlike us, it's without dreams.

The aliens there are very kind,
But one or two were slightly blind.

Although I know this doesn't matter,
But did you know that Mars is flatter?

In a special surrounding zone,
Our spaceship flew like it's never flown.

Fast, free and not even blown.

Felicity Andrews (9)
The Red Maids' Junior School

SUN

Cold shivering eye,
Icy winds are my breath,
When I cry I send floods,
When I sigh I send tornadoes,
When I am angry I send volcanoes
My cold, clipped laughter. I am valiant,
My winds are like a rapier.

I kidnap the world
It all belongs to me.
My passionate beauty will startle you,
My glowing face will blind you,
Yet when I look down on my people
How I wish I was one of them.

My venomous and malicious heart
Changes the whole world,
I am king over all
Mountains bow to me.

Gazing over the world waiting for my death
It is near, in the year 1,000,000.

I watch my brothers and sisters fall
Saturn, Mars, Jupiter and Uranus,
And all the rest,
But me.

Now it is my turn
Down,
Down.

I take away light, warmth, joy
Nothing dark, hills, tunnels
Where does it end
This ever-going path of despair?

Georgina Brooke (10)
The Red Maids' Junior School

WHITE TIGER'S PAIN

He had sadness filling up his eyes,
Staring not caring if he lives or dies
Back and forth he strides, back and forth he strides,
Rocking his body from side to side.

In a tiny little food dish he had,
Dried up meat covered in flies,
Up and down he pads, up and down he pads,
The empty water dish leaves a thirst he cannot hide.

The mate staring at me through her sharp red eyes,
And keeps her dead cub close by,
Still has her pride, still has her pride,
She has a sadness in her face that cannot be denied.

The dead cub with its mummy,
Still sad even though it's dead,
Backwards and forwards he runs, backwards and forwards he runs,
The mummy's paw resting on its head.

Holly Barrington (10)
The Red Maids' Junior School

SHAMU

Shamu is a killer whale
When he jumped out
He splashed me with his tail
Then he squirted water about.

He lives in San Diego
Sea World is his home
Read the notices when you go
And don't sit in the wet zone.

Cos if you do
You'll get a soak
Splashed, sprayed or squirted
It is no joke.

Fine fins flickering
Smooth blubbery skin
Under the water glistening
As he happily swims.

Hannah Miller (9)
The Red Maids' Junior School

THE LIONESS

A golden mane, flashing in the darkness,
An almighty roar, heard from miles around,
A puzzled face, wondering if there's a likeness,
Between her, her prey and her hunter.

Trained ears, listening to the strange sounds,
Sharp claws, her paws padding the ground,
Cutting eyes, looking at lots of termite mounds,
Looking as cuddly as a teddy bear.

But she ruins masses of hard work on crops,
She destroys a lifetime of raising animals,
She scares all men who dare trespass on her rocks,
Yes, she may seem cute and cuddly, but inside
She is a killer.

Charlotte Juckes (8)
The Red Maids' Junior School

MY PETS

My cat
Has the ears of a bat
And to add to that
He's very fat.

My dog
Snores like a hog
Sleeps like a log
Bounces like my frog.

My ferret
Just can't bear it
Would like a fish
Oh how I wish.

My rabbit
Sees food he grabs it.
My guinea pig
As thin as a twig.

My parrot
Same colour as a carrot.
My hamster
Has escaped.

Pippa Smith (8)
The Red Maids' Junior School

THE SEA

The bright, blue sea is the place for me
Twinkling silver in the sun
The seagull swoops and loops the loop
While the white waves crash below, below,
While the white waves crash below.

The bright, blue sea is the place for me
Twinkling silver in the sun
The dolphin leaps and jumps and spins
While the white waves crash around, around
While the white waves crash around.

The bright, blue sea is the place for me
Twinkling silver in the sun
The fishes swim and turn their fins
While the white waves crash above, above
While the white waves crash above.

Alexandra Wilkinson (10)
The Red Maids' Junior School

I DON'T WANT TO . . .

I don't want to . . .
Get up,
Tie my laces,
Go to school,
Do PE,
Go to Brownies
Or
Do my homework,
I only want to stay at home
And watch TV.

Laura Currie (9)
The Red Maids' Junior School

MY BABY SISTER

I was on the garden chair
Holding a gooey, wet and disgusting baby sister on my lap
I hate her!

Her name was Dolly
Dolly is my worst name
She's disgusting!

She is much worse than my big sister Katie
Who is really mean
I don't like it!

Mum and Dad came out with the camera
I groaned 'Yuck' a picture of *me* and Dolly
I don't like her!

Click
Went the camera.

Naomi Warbutton (8)
The Red Maids' Junior School

MY SISTER

My sister,
Is a blister,
She drives me insane,
She is a big pain.
No one can resist my sister,
Because no one likes her,
I think she can hear,
Oh dear!

Stephanie Ting (11)
The Red Maids' Junior School

ANIMALS OF THIS WORLD

Monkeys swinging through the trees,
Eagles swooping in the breeze.
Lions roaring in the plain,
Dogs leaping through the rain.

Pigs grunting, soaked in mud,
Cows sitting, chewing cud.
Dolphins jumping over the seas
Hedgehogs scratching off their fleas.

Think of animals everywhere,
On ground, in water and in air.
Some are beautiful, useful or clever,
Keep them safe forever and ever.

Sarah Bedford (10)
The Red Maids' Junior School

MY PETS

Rabbits and guinea pigs
Are very nice pets
You hardly take them to the vets
When you have a dog or cat
You always find them on a mat
Apart from dogs which are pretty cool
You always find them with a ball.
But when the parrots come to play
Take it from me and run away
Snails and tortoises are very cool pets
But you will find they can't handle the vet's
When the night falls they all go to bed
Apart from the cat who stays outside instead.

Alice Wait (10)
Two Mile Hill Junior School

MATHS

Maths is terrible
I've got a test in three weeks
I stole the answer book
To take a few peeks
That didn't help
Didn't help at all
My mark will be one out of ten
That isn't good at all
I'll pretend to be sick
Mash cornflakes with beans
I'll get excluded from school
I'll go wearing jeans
But I'll just have to face up
That I've got a test
Don't think my marks will be one of the best.

Cody Clarke (9)
Two Mile Hill Junior School

HOT AND COLD

Hot and cold cannot live together.
Cold is like an icy lake.
Hot is like a summer's evening.
Cold is like rain on your cheek.
Hot is like a barbecue.
Cold despises you, for heating up a fire.
Hot is a warm fire waiting for you in the stove.
Cold is a freezer but it doesn't shut out the warm.
Hot is like a holiday on the beach.
Cold is like a snow storm.
Hot is like a devil.
Cold is like an angel.

Stacey Bond (10)
Two Mile Hill Junior School

BAD MORNING

My alarm is dinging,
My sister is singing,
And my doorbell keeps on ringing.

I'm getting dressed,
While my brother's being a pest,
And my mum and dad are playing chess.

My sister's reading her post,
My mum is cooking our toast,
But my brother wants the most.

My mum is writing a tag,
I'm picking up my bag,
While my brother is falling down the stairs in his sleeping bag.

My sister is a state,
My brother wants to bake a cake,
You can tell I'm gonna be late!

Michaela Churchill (11)
Two Mile Hill Junior School

I WANT TO BE A STAR

I want to be a star
And play a big guitar
In front of those screaming kids
I hope we'll go so far.

But we haven't got a name
Oh what a shame
Shall we go without
Or shall we call us Fame?

But we haven't got a song
Now it's going wrong
Perhaps we should go home
That won't take very long.

I don't want to be a star
Don't want to play guitar
Because my mum and dad
Say you're fine the way you are.

Claire Short (9)
Two Mile Hill Junior School

CLOTHES ADVENTURE

Last night I went on a clothes adventure
I really don't know where,
First I had a shopping spree
Then I did my hair.

Then I went into a place
Named The Music Centre,
Here was a glittery sign on the door
It had in big writing, 'Enter'!

Then I went in the tie-dye shop
With seven pounds for a skirt
But in the end I ended up buying
A really nice bright red shirt.

Then I went to the lift
And I pressed the buttoned door
Instead of taking me to the mall
I landed on my bedroom floor.

Nikita Shellard (9)
Two Mile Hill Junior School

CAN'T RESIST CHOCOLATE

'Mummy, there's a box of chocolates on the table,
Can I have some please?'
'No'
'But please Mummy they look:
Great,
Fab,
Wicked,
Cool,
Ace,
Super,
Wonderful,
Amazing,
Fabulous,
Marvellous,
Exceptional,
Thrilling,
Gripping,
Mouth-watering,
Tasty
'Burp - *Oops* sorry Mum, they're all gone!'

Hannah Bloomfield (10)
Two Mile Hill Junior School

THE GIRL AND THE DOG

The girl
Got stuck
When she
Fell in the muck.

She called
For her dog
Who was wandering
In the fog.

The dog
Got stopped
By the cop
Who had just shopped.

The girl
Had short hair
Which was covered in mud,
She didn't care.

Louise Atwell (9)
Two Mile Hill Junior School

DREAMS

One warm sunny day,
As I sat by the river,
I dreamed of somewhere far away.

I drifted away
To a fairytale land
With unicorns leaping
On the golden sands.

Of magical lands
And heroic adventures
Where birds sing
In total harmony.

One warm sunny day
As I sat by the river,
I dreamed of somewhere far away.

Kirsty Raynard (10)
Two Mile Hill Junior School

LINE DANCING

Line dancing is very good fun.

Everyone stands in a line, trying to keep time,
By moving their feet to the sound of the beat.

Line dancing is very good fun.

Wearing cowboy hats and boots made of hide,
They all shimmy and chase from side to side.

Line dancing is very good fun.

They kick ball change with a stamp and a clap,
They hitch their knee and give it a slap.

Line dancing is very good fun.
It's not at all difficult but easily done.

Hollie Atwell (11)
Two Mile Hill Junior School

THE CREATURE

The creature stepped into my garden
Its great feet made footprints
I watched as the mud hardened
It stared at me not blinking.

I shivered
I waited for its next move
But to my surprise it quivered
And picked up the half eaten chicken.

As it left it winked
Its hairy eyes fixed on me
I went pink
As I watched it leave.

Tanya Trott (11)
Two Mile Hill Junior School

PAIN

I'm a pain
I'm going insane
I don't know what to do
I am quite sad
I'm going mad
And I wish I hadn't the flu!

I have a clogged nose,
I don't like those
And my chest is very weary
I hate my mum
She thinks I'm her son
And when she calls me deary!

But I love my dad,
He makes me glad,
I live to see the daylight
But my mum
I'd smack her bum,
And be grounded if I had to!

So this is how my poem ends,
I don't think anything's going to change,
Do you?

Sidonie Monks (9)
Two Mile Hill Junior School

THE MERMAID

A loud noise came from the great sea,
A diver came diving out of a boat made of green peas,
Under the water he saw a beautiful girl,
She was wearing a long pretty pearl.
He swam up to her and saw a fish,
The fish was wearing a seaweed dish,
She started to sing a lovely song,
Then suddenly he heard a big gong.
The girl started to laugh with joy,
As she pulled out a beautiful toy,
This was no toy it was a treasure,
It was made out of gold, and sixteen centimetres was its measure.
The diver swam nearer and nearer,
While the mermaid was looking in her mirror,
Then suddenly she heard a scream,
She rushed home and realised it was a dream.
She swam back to the place where she met the diver,
And found his wallet, and inside it was a fiver,
The diver came diving back down, and saw the girl,
With the very long pearl.
Then suddenly she swam far, far away,
The diver came back every day,
And he never saw the mermaid ever again.

Cherelle Williamson-Grey (9)
Two Mile Hill Junior School

MY BEST FRIEND

My best friend Ryan Appleford drives me up the wall
Usually we go out and play some football
If we're not playing football we're playing a war
Most of the time he's hiding by the back door
When we play our war games I always take a chance
Ryan is a wimp he's even scared of ants.

But I like Ryan Appleford for the person that he is
His smiling face, his cheeky grin and the show-off he is
Each morning in the register I listen for his call
But he's always running late and is never on the ball
I know Miss Barton thinks he's a pest
But I like Ryan Appleford because he is the best.

Daniel Crossman (9)
Two Mile Hill Junior School

ALIENS

Aliens are like an unsolved mystery
They have their own lunar civilisation
Whilst we only have a NASA station,
They soar all day to far away galaxies
We only can dream of the possibilities
We look for rock samples,
Compared to us they are the super beings
We are the Neanderthals!

Cassie Lynett (10)
Two Mile Hill Junior School

HIPPOPOTAMUS

Hippopotamus never
Puts boots on in rainy weather
To slosh in mud up to ears
Brings great joy and merry tears
Their pleasure lies in being messed up
They just won't play at being dressed up
In fact a swamp is a heaven plus
If you're a hippopotamus!

Hannah Anderson (11)
Two Mile Hill Junior School

My Rabbit, Daisy

My pet rabbit is called daisy
She's fun, mischievous and crazy
When she doesn't want her food
She tosses it away
When we sort out her hutch we put in lots of hay.
My sister's rabbit is called Lucky
He likes to play with his rubber ducky
Daisy is six months, Lucky is three months old
We keep them in the garage, outdoors is cold
Gemma has seen them, Jasmine and Hollie
The dog Jessie won't see them or Mollie.
Lucky likes sitting on my dad's motorbike
Now you sort of know what our rabbits are like.

Katherine Reid (9)
Two Mile Hill Junior School

Tortoise And Hare

'Tortoise! Tortoise! Were you there?
Tell me what happened between you and the hare?
Did you win or did you lose?
Or did you cry those baby blues?
The time has come I need to know
Were you fast or were you slow?
So tell me what happened was it you or the hare
I need to know because I care.'

'Yes my friend I will tell
I had the race with my friend hare
He got so tired he lost the race
I guess he couldn't keep up with my quick pace.'

Ben Ford (11)
Two Mile Hill Junior School

ANGELS AND DEVILS

Angels are heavenly.
Devils are evil.
Angels are like a happy face looking down on you.
Devils are like immaculate guns waiting for the right moment to shoot.
Angels are perfect in every single way.
Devils are putrid carrying sick around.
Angels are like a medicine cure.
Devils are like naughty little boys.
Angels are statues in the holy church.
Devils are like big bullies.
Angels are like strong body guards.
Devils are like mischief makers.
Angels are Christians and trust in God.
Devils are the opposite.

Kelly Panes (10)
Two Mile Hill Junior School

BEST NAN IN THE WHOLE WIDE WORLD

You're the best nan in the world
No one is better than you
You're special to me because . . .
You try your best in everything,
You are caring and respectful,
You are kind and gentle,
And always careful,
And that's six reasons why I love you
You're the best nan in the whole wide world
And I will never forget you.

Rebecca Davis (10)
Two Mile Hill Junior School

TOYS

Toys, toys, everywhere
Some are round and some are square.

Some are active and some are not.

Some toys have arms and legs and others are just wooden pegs.

Some go fast, others slow
Some you play in the snow
Others you blow to score a goal
Others you might take to school.

Some are big, others are small
But there is one thing important
You can play with them all.

Matthew Stone (11)
Two Mile Hill Junior School

WEATHER

The rain is lashing down on my windowpane
'Oh no, here is the rain again.'

Sun, it tries to shine,
But through the cloud it fails,
I want to go out
But the path is full of snails.

Hannah Tucker (10)
Two Mile Hill Junior School

MY BROTHER

My brother is so annoying,
He wakes up early every morning,
We always fight,
He thinks he is the best,
He gets little credit,
And I get the rest.

Oh and I forgot to tell you,
His name is Liam,
And when we have to take things to school,
He nearly always forgets 'em.

Hollie Wedmore (9)
Two Mile Hill Junior School

THE GIRAFFE

My giraffe has . . .
Skin as orange and yellow as sunset,
Hair on neck as golden snow,
The ears as pointy as a church spire,
Head like two big footballs,
Eyes as wide as the ocean,
Joints in legs as big as pebbles,
Spots as dotty as a child with measles,
Tail as short as my finger,
Long legs as thin as a branch,
Body as fast as giant rocks and stones.

This giraffe is an African giraffe.

Georgina Sellars (9)
Victoria Park Junior School

ZIBS

Beware!
Beware!
The zibs are there.
They are hairy,
They are scary,
They are incredibly ferocious.
They have greasy hair
And a nasty stare
They sometimes smell quite atrocious.
They do not swear
And they never care
And they are quite delicious.
Beware!
Beware!
The zibs are there.
Beware!
Beware!
The zibs are there.

Shona O'Halloran (10)
Victoria Park Junior School

GIRAFFE

Giraffe, giraffe hiding in the trees,
While walking fast through the chilling breeze,
Hear the trees swish and sway,
Giraffe, giraffe laying on the bay,
Giraffe, giraffe eating a banana,
But why don't giraffes wear their pyjamas?

Roxanne Clarke (11)
Victoria Park Junior School

CHEETAH

Cheetah
Flash of fur,
Flick of tail,
Cheetah.

Pounding of paws,
Flicking of legs,
Cheetah.

Blur of spots,
Crunch of dry grass,
Cheetah.

Arched shoulders,
Take down an antelope,
Cheetah!

Eve Andreski (9)
Victoria Park Junior School

IMAGINE

Imagine a flea as big as my knee.
Imagine a cup as big as a duck.
Imagine a sail as big as a whale.
Imagine me as big as a tree.
Imagine nests as big as Jess.
Imagine a dot as big as a clock.
Imagine a dog as big as a log.
Imagine the sea as small as an ant.

Danielle Barnes (9)
Victoria Park Junior School

I Wish . . .

I wish leaves were as big as trees.

I wish Lindy was more like Sindy.

I wish you could hold the cold.

When there's a draft, we all laugh.

When it's winter I get a splinter.

When I'm near trees I always sneeze.

I wish the rain wasn't a pain.

I wish the snow would flow.

I wish my uniform was nice and warm.

Melissa Deady (8)
Victoria Park Junior School

Dophins

When I see a dolphin it makes me want to play with them all day.
Even though I've never seen one, I dream about them every night
And this is what I imagine,
I imagine that they're slippery, wet, friendly and funny, graceful
                                                      and beautiful
I imagine their lovely sounds
Also shiny, playful, all blue
It makes me happy to think of that.

Roisin Brown (9)
Victoria Park Junior School

NUMBER POEM

One naughty nit, nudged its nose,
Two terrible tigers, tickled their toes.

Three kicking kangaroos, kicked the king,
Four rubbish rats, ripped a ring.

Five chatting cheetahs, caught a cat,
Six big badgers, bit a bat.

Seven bad babies, broke the bed,
Eight happy hippos, hurt their heads.

Nine big brothers, brought a boat,
Ten cuddly cats, wore a coat.

Matthew Hodge (9)
Victoria Park Junior School

AUTUMN

Autumn is the time to wrap up warm
Chilly breeze,
Blowing leaves,
Whistling winds,
Fluttering leaves
Young children playing in the park, in the dark, green leaves
Parents drinking hot cups of coffee
Wearing woolly hats, scarves and gloves
Autumn is cold with a bright sky, but a blustering breeze.

Jade Prudhoe (9)
Victoria Park Junior School

SNOW

When I looked out of my bedroom window,
I saw a blanket of snow on the ground,
Then I looked up to the sky,
Little white dots were falling to the ground,
I ran downstairs and put my shoes and coat on.
The door was open so I jumped out into the snow,
It was a cold, windy morning,
It was frosty,
It was windy.
I heard the ice crackling beneath my feet as I walked on top of it.

Alix Tucker (8)
Victoria Park Junior School

DOLPHINS

Dolphins are grey, smooth and wet
I am going to place a bet.
They play in the water
They dance and they sing
I wish I had one wing.
They can kill sharks
Sharks can kill them.
Dolphins are friendly
We are friendly to them.
Their shows are good
I want to adopt one.

Alex Thomson (10)
Victoria Park Junior School

STARS

There are . . .
Bright stars,
White stars,
And glowing stars too.
I like stars they make me feel cold like gold.
There are more stars like . . .
Shooting star by the hooting owls,
Some stars to be seen, some stars not to be seen.
Fancy stars bowing down to you!

Rachel McGinn (9)
Victoria Park Junior School

WILD CATS

Wild cats, wild cats chase after their prey
This animal needs to move so fast
The puma's coat is grey, grey, grey
Puma, puma you run so far
Make your speed last, last, last.

Amy Pinchen (11)
Victoria Park Junior School

THE TIGER

Tiger, tiger looking for meat,
While sniffing at their smelly feet,
As they rush to get their prey
In the morning and in the day.

Louise Purnell (11)
Victoria Park Junior School

A MAGIC SPELL

Ingredients:
Two stars that have fallen from the sky,
Wind captured in a jar,
Ten pines from a pine tree,
One pint of water from a stream,
Twenty hailstones.

Method:
Catch two sparkling stars from the sky
Chop them up and leave them to dry.
Shake the wind in its jar,
Make a wish from your heart.
Take the pines, shake them in your hand,
Put them in the jar and put on the ground.
Add the water, mix very well,
Sprinkle the stars with the hail.
Freeze the ingredients for an hour or so,
Then let it melt and let it go.
Watch it twirl and whirl in the sky,
Think of me and close your eyes.

Anna Webb (10)
Wellesley Primary School

THE TIGER

The tiger is angry.
The tiger is fierce.
The tiger is scary.
The tiger is grumpy.
The tiger is stripy.
The tiger is yellow.
The tiger is *mad*.

Amy Collins (7)
Wellesley Primary School

WINGS

If I had wings
I would dance on the sun's rays
That shine on me.

If I had wings
I would taste the moon
As cold as ice cream.

If I had wings
I would travel through space
And meet all of the planets.

If I had wings
I would listen to the peaceful wind
That speeds past me.

If I had wings
I would play football
With all the angels in Heaven.

Fernando Martinez-Cowles (9)
Wellesley Primary School

WOOD

Owls screech,
Trees swish,
Grass whispers,
Birds tweet,
Woodpeckers crash,
Butterflies flash,
Crows pick the worms out of the ground!

Zachary Witney (7)
Wellesley Primary School

RECIPE FOR MAGIC

Ingredients:
One star,
One feather
Three petals,
Twenty-five raindrops.

Hold a feather in the sky, blow three times and let it fly.

Find the brightest star you see, hold it tight and think of me.

Raindrops falling everywhere, make sure that you get wet hair.

The smelliest smell you've ever smelt, squeeze it tight and let it melt.

Now you've worked out how it's done
I'll make sure you get there, so no harm's done.

Kelly Hicks, Sarah Hall & Lauren Cooper (10)
Wellesley Primary School

LIONS ROAR

At the zoo
Lions roar, seals sniff,
Children shout!

At the farm
Cows moo, horses whinny,
The farmer works.

At home
Dad annoys me,
I talk,
Mum says . . .
'I'm a princess!'

Alice Juggins (7)
Wellesley Primary School

WINGS

If I had wings
I would fly through space
And play football with the stars.

If I had wings
I would fly to a faraway galaxy
And meet the people on Ratooine.

If I had wings
I would listen to the angels sing their songs.

If I had wings
I would play basketball with ghosts.

George Gibson (8)
Wellesley Primary School

FEAR

I was fearful and shocked,
And it seemed that my guts had frozen solid
And as I got whiter and whiter,
My guts got colder and colder,
I was in a trance,
Then I began to see colours,
Like black and red,
Then as I got whiter and whiter
The walls started moving in, trying to crush me,
They got closer and closer every second
It was terrible.

Sebastian Whiteford (9)
Wick CE Primary School

SAD

I was angry and mad
And it seemed that my heart was broken
And as I got sadder and sadder
My heart got smaller and smaller
I was upset
Then I began to see colours
Like red and black
Then I was sad
I began to cry
I did not like it
I wished it would stop
I was screaming with sadness
Nobody could help
My mother could not help me
Then it was over
I was sad.

Amy Skinner (9)
Wick CE Primary School

SNOW

Snow is falling in the air
Children playing everywhere
Snowballs going here and there
We go sledging over there
Making igloos in the field
A big snowman shall we build
Pack the snow up nice and tight
Come on kids let's get it right.

Stephen Thomas (9)
Wick CE Primary School

SAD

I was heartbroken and depressed
My heart was hollow and empty,
And as I got glummer and glummer,
I got lonelier and lonelier all the time,
I was in misery,
Then I began to see colours,
Like blue and black
Then as I got more depressed,
I felt I was in a deserted room,
On my own with nobody,
It was dreadful,
And it would not stop
I was burning in misery
I was so upset
No one could stop me.

Stuart Cranfield (10)
Wick CE Primary School

THE FARM AND COUNTRY

The smell of fried breakfast.
The sweet singing birds flying from tree to tree.
The gentle breezes blowing the trees and hedges.
The sound of tractors working in the distance.
Trees dotted all over the fields.
The dribbling of the water in the tank in the yard.
The farm dog getting muddy, running through the dirty puddles
And barking when a car goes past.

Sam Kidner (10)
Wick CE Primary School

SADNESS

I was down in the dumps
It seemed there was a child wanting his mum inside me
And as I got gloomier and gloomier
The baby was wailing harder and harder
It was terrible
Then I began to see shades of colour
Like red and black
I was really unhappy
I felt like I was shot in the back
Blood was running down my dress
It was revolting,
And it wouldn't stop
I was streaming with sadness
Nobody could stop me
My mother could not stop me,
Then it went,
I felt much better when it had gone
Just horrible, coloured, sadness.

Elicia Prophet (10)
Wick CE Primary School

JUST IMAGINE

Imagine if you could fly
Right up into the sky
Inside a cardboard box
Or if you could walk through walls
Without any cuts or knocks!

If hens had four legs,
And puppies had two
Or if wandering ghosts came round
Woo! Woo!

If pigs could fly,
High in the sky
Or if truth could lie
Well,
Just think what could happen.

Betsy Hayward (10)
Wick CE Primary School

LONELY

I was single and solitary,
And it seemed I was on a cloud,
And as I got more withdrawn
The sky delivered something grey, something loud,
I was vibrating with fright
Then I began to see flowers
Some black and wrinkled, some pink and purple
But as I calmed down
The flowers began to bloom,
They were slipping into a shape,
It was colossal I assumed
And it didn't want to pause,
I could see the flowers' claws,
Nobody could stop me,
Just those flowers saying 'Pot me'
Who is that shape just like an ape?
It is my mother munching grapes,
It was gone,
Mum sang a song,
I am alright,
With no bright light
New, flowery, frills.

Rachael Iles (9)
Wick CE Primary School

UNHAPPY

I was getting down and down
And it seemed that I'd gone to the Second World War
And as I felt down and down
And it seemed that the Second World War got dangerous and dangerous
I was in gloom
I began to see guns and grenades being fired out of trenches
Like rifles and grenades
Then I felt down and down
My heart pumping faster than ever
It was pumping too fast and popping
And it kept rebuilding itself back to normal and dropping.
It was like that a dog ate your heart and it wouldn't stop
And it wouldn't go away.

Jonny Filer (9)
Wick CE Primary School

SKY

A vast expanse of space and air with no beginning or end,
In summertime lying on my back, time easily I can spend,
Watching pure white clouds drifting lazily across an ocean of blue
With birds, butterflies and bees all busily flying through.

In winter its dark grey colour holds promises of snow,
North winds toss the birds about,
Where the sun's gone I don't know!

What is sky?

Samuel Pegler (10)
Wick CE Primary School

SADNESS

I was sad and emotional
And it seemed my heart was being ripped out by some form of evil
And as I began to degenerate more and more
The evil began to pierce worse and worse
I was down in the dumps
Then I began to see colours
Like blue and red
Then as I began to get what seemed fully declined
My body fell into a pit of nightmares
They wreaked havoc among me,
It was startling,
And it wouldn't dare stop
I was wailing with tears,
Nobody could cheer me
My mother couldn't cheer me
Then like a flash it stopped,
I was once again fine.

Ben Tovey-Cowley (10)
Wick CE Primary School

SADNESS

I was sad and upset
It seemed that the world was coming to an end,
And as I got worried more and more,
Then it seemed that the world had turned its back on me,
I was hurt,
Then I began to see colours,
Like blue and brown,
Then as I got sadder and sadder,
I heard one hundred people shouting at me inside my head,
The shouting got louder and louder.

Victoria Gregory (9)
Wick CE Primary School

EMBARRASSED

I was shocked and angry,
It seemed like everyone was laughing at me
My heart was pounding with stress,
I felt like I was in a cage,
Then I began to see colours
Like red and grey,
Then as I got more embarrassed
My ears were streaming with redness
They sounded like trains going 'Cho, cho'
It was so terrible
And it would not stop
I was in a horrible nightmare
Nobody could stop me, being embarrassed
My mother could not stop me,
Then it had all gone
And I was all right,
Nice, normal, fun.

Sarah Baggs (9)
Wick CE Primary School

MUM

You cook my tea and wash my clothes,
You tell me off when I am bad,
You help me when I'm stuck at school,
You cuddle me when I'm sad.

You praise me when I get things right,
You let me have lots of fun,
You buy me sweets and lots of toys,
You're a special mum.

Katrina Wares (9)
Wick CE Primary School

EMBARRASSED

I was so humiliated
Then I was hot under the collar,
As I was more shown-up
I got hotter and hotter under the collar,
Then I was in the dumps,
After I began to see figures,
Of all the happy times instead of now,
My heart was beating a dreadful tune,
Like it lost a friend,
It was appalling,
And it wouldn't go,
I was so livid,
I couldn't stop myself,
My sister tried to calm me down,
Then it went
I was fine
Awful, terrible, humiliation.

William Adams (9)
Wick CE Primary School

MY HAMSTER MILO

I got a new hamster yesterday,
And he plays all day,
And his name is Milo,
He is black and cuddly,
As he runs in his spinning wheel he occasionally looks up at you,
And he eats like a small pig,
He is crunchy and munchy.

Liam Hargreaves (9)
Wick CE Primary School

THE SEA SNAKE

Slowly,
Silently,
Smoothly,
Slithering,
Over the
Smooth,
White
Sand.
The sea snake
Slipped
Towards
The shore.
His
Scaly body
Shimmered
In the
Warm
Sunlight.
The
Sand
Was
Too hot
For
Him
So he
Searched
For
The
Safety
Of the
Sea
Back where he belonged.

Elizabeth Land (9)
Wick CE Primary School

BEWARE

Beware! Beware! Of this terrible bear,
It will pull you by the strings
Of your hair.
It will munch you here
And munch you there.
So please, beware, beware of this terrible bear.

Beware! Beware! Of this terrible cave,
In which a giant monster
Will wade.
He's even known to set many a grave,
So please, beware, beware of this terrible cave.

Oliver Woodman (9)
Wick CE Primary School

MY BEST FRIEND

I have a friend
Who is kind and true
We stick together
Like a pot of glue.

I have a friend
We do lots together
I hope we will be
Friends forever.

I have a friend
Of whom I'm a fan.
I have a friend
And his name is Dan.

Ben Watts (10)
Wick CE Primary School

SAD

I was lonely and sad
And it seemed there was cold water inside me
And as I got sadder and sadder
The water got colder and colder
I was so unhappy
Then I began to see colours
Like grey and blue
Then as I got more mournful and mournful
I began to feel weak
Then I began to feel weaker than before
It was scary
I could not stop feeling weak
I was weeping with sadness
Nobody could stop me
My sister could not stop me
Then I stopped feeling weak
And I was fine.

Emma Roch (9)
Wick CE Primary School